For Jews and for Christians, the notion of blessing is bound up with praising God and giving thanks to God; bound up with our way of seeing, understanding, and being in this world and in the human community. The prayer of blessing is part of our heritage from Judaism, and it continues to be a living part of Jewish life today.

Bishops' Committee on the Liturgy, NCCB
Catholic Household Blessings & Prayers, 1988, p. 16

I think of you, Jesus, who couldn't bear the idea of leaving us. You, in solidarity with humanity, the perfect lover, at the end of the terrestrial platform. You made a gesture – the sharing of bread and wine – and through it you said: 'I renew my alliance. I give myself to the Father and I give myself to you.' You, Jesus, put your entire being into that gesture and you made us a promise – that every time we re-enact it, you will be among us in a real total way. And we will enter into communion with one another and become, together, the Body which must continue to grow to the end of time.

Quoist, *With Open Heart*, 1986, pp. 157f.

At the source of the Christian liturgy lies the Jewish liturgy.

Deiss, *Springtime of the Liturgy*, 1979, p. 3

Take, Bless, Break, Share

Simon Bryden-Brook has an Anglican and a Roman Catholic background, including theological studies at Westcott House and Catholic University in Washington DC, and is secretary of the European Network Church on the Move.

Take, Bless, Break, Share

Agapes, Table Blessings
and other
Small Group Liturgies

edited by
Simon Bryden-Brook

CANTERBURY
PRESS
Norwich

Text © in this compilation Simon Bryden-Brook
and Catholics for a Changing Church 1998
14 West Halkin Street, London SW1X 8JS

Illustrations © Paul M. Jenkins 1998

First published in 1998 by The Canterbury Press Norwich
(a publishing imprint of Hymns Ancient & Modern Limited
a registered charity)
St Mary's Works, St Mary's Plain
Norwich, Norfolk NR3 3BH

British Library Cataloguing in Publication Data

A catalogue record for this book is available
from the British Library

ISBN 1-85311-214-3

Typeset by David Gregson Associates, Beccles, Suffolk
and printed in Great Britain by
Biddles Ltd, Guildford and King's Lynn

Contents

Contents

Contents

indicates liturgies with the words of institution, see pp. xii.

Preface

This work represents almost thirty years of Christian celebration by small Christian communities in England. More specifically, the liturgies presented here were composed or adapted from published sources, by members of the Catholic Renewal Movement (CRM), now called Catholics for a Changing Church. CRM was founded in January 1969 as a 'grass-roots' organization by a number of Roman Catholics who were dissatisfied by the leadership offered by their Church at that time. Its members have been labelled 'dissident' Catholics and are ready to admit that they have often felt marginalized by the structures of the Church. As a result, most of these liturgies do not enjoy ecclesiastical approval; it has never been sought and never desired. They have been prepared by lay people for lay people, and our priest members have always played a secondary role, as their official position requires.

Although essentially a practical work, inevitably some technical expressions are used and for this reason a Glossary (see p. 161) is provided. Reference to the published work of liturgical scholars has been kept to the minimum, but a short bibliography is supplied for those interested in examining the origins of Christian liturgy and the Eucharist in particular (p. 175).

A section entitled Practical Points follows the Introduction, designed to explain how to organize a table blessing or other small group liturgy. Users of this book are free to adapt these liturgies as they wish. Some of the language might seem dated or exclusive today, for example. Liturgies which make use of the eucharistic words of institution are marked with an asterisk (*). Some modern Other Resources are also listed (see in particular *Catholic Household Blessings & Prayers* (NCCB/USCC, Washington DC, 1988), John Henson, *Other Communions of Jesus* (Stantonbury Parish Print, 1994) and John Vincent (ed.), *Community Worship Revised* (Ashram Community Trust, Sheffield, 1987)).

Fuller notes on Sources and Acknowledgements are also printed on pages 165–72. Unfortunately, not all the sources of the liturgies in this collection are known. Readers are asked to write and let us know if they can assist in providing more information. Where liturgies are taken from or based on published texts, then due acknowledgement is made, where we are aware of this. If we have inadvertently breached anyone's copyright, we apologize and shall make appropriate acknowledgement in future editions. Specific acknowledgement is made for quotations from *The Jerusalem Bible* (published and © 1966, 1967 and 1968 by Darton, Longman and Todd and Doubleday, and used by permission of the publishers), and *The Grail Psalms (An Inclusive Language Version)* (William Collins).

As compiler and editor of this collection, I am well aware how many people have contributed to this work over the years. The Spirit has chosen a variety of instruments. I recall particularly John Eaton of Birmingham University who, in 1966–8, first opened my eyes to the riches of Hebrew thought and the Jewish traditions we share, at a time when the consequences of Vatican II's *Constitution on the Sacred Liturgy* had scarcely begun to sink in. In 1968 too, Hamish Swanston, later Professor of Theology at the University of Kent, opened my eyes to the limitations of much teaching on the Eucharist in a paper provocatively entitled 'From picnic to High Mass and back again!' In 1989, when I was fortunate enough to be able to attend a course of her lectures, Professor Mary Collins OSB of the Catholic University in Washington DC stimulated my interest in the origins of the Eucharist.

Above all however, I pay tribute to my mentor of over thirty years, John Challenor, who by his self-effacing but inspiring ministry has brought me to understand the psalmist and the author of the Letter to the Hebrews: *Tu es sacerdos in aeternum* (Ps. 110:4 [LXX 109] and Heb. 5:6). To him this work is respectfully and affectionately dedicated by the editor and Catholics for a Changing Church, in whose foundation he was instrumental and whose Chair he has latterly occupied with distinction.

The members of the house church in London to which I belong, and which meets twice monthly for table fellowship, discussion, celebration and prayer, have also contributed much to this collection in the past few years. This collection is used by them and they offer it freely to fellow Christians in the hope that it will encourage them to meet and worship in this special way.

In addition particular thanks are due to St Deiniol's Library, Hawarden, Clwyd, which, by awarding me a short scholarship to work in its ecumenical and stimulating atmosphere, provided me with the time, the freedom and the opportunity to prepare this collection for publication. Of course, none of those mentioned are in any way responsible for opinions expressed in this work, any errors or imperfections.

Simon Bryden-Brook
All Saints, 1997

Introduction

*This book contains a collection of liturgies for celebra-
tion at home, without the need for an ordained minister
to be present. Most of them are agapes, a revival of an
ancient Christian custom of table fellowship.*

The Body of Christ

If Jesus Christ is indeed God's presence in the world and if he
has called all women and men to share in his redeeming
work, then the Eucharist is central. The Eucharist is in fact
not only the presence of Christ in the bread and wine but the
presence of the Risen Christ in the Christian community
gathered together to celebrate and *effect the reality of the
presence of God* in our own spheres of influence. So the
central message of Christianity is a simple one: God is to be
found in humankind and it is through humankind that the
world is to be transformed. Jesus Christ is the primordial
sacrament of God's presence in the world, and it is the human
Church, celebrating this in the Eucharist as the Body of the
Risen Christ, that is called to be God's redeeming presence in
our world today.

But formulations such as these rarely themselves communicate the message. This failure to communicate the gospel in
language capable of speaking to modern men and women is
mirrored in the inability of the Church to allow her sacra-
ments to convey their message. The recent abandonment of
Latin as the common liturgical language of the Western
Catholic Church was only one, certainly major, step forward.
This criticism applies essentially to the Eucharist, the very
sacrament of Christ's saving presence. It has become a

mysterious church service, presided over by clergy and only fully understood by the initiated. The bread is often almost perversely sacralized to the point of unrecognizability and the celebration frequently obscured by hymns, bizarre conventions, strange language and unnatural postures.

An understanding of this centrality in theology of the Eucharist is not easily gained by regular attendance at our celebrations in church. These so often obscure the essentials. This is one of the reasons why a number of Christians, forming themselves into small communities, sometimes called House Churches or Basic Christian Communities (Intentional or Small Christian Communities are some of the many other terms used), have over the past thirty years in particular sought to improve their understanding by cele-brating at home or in some other secular environment.

Returning to a neglected tradition

This central significance in Christian teaching of the Eucharist as both a sign and the means of realizing Christ's presence in our world today is not the only reason for the growth of table celebrations among Christians. There is also a deliberate intention of reviving a pre-Eucharist tradition, which has indeed been obscured by the development of the Eucharist as we know it today.

Food and drink feature in all religions, from libations and offerings of food, such as rice and milk, to ceremonial banquets with formal toasts afterwards. The centre of Christian worship too is a meal, the Lord's supper or Eucharist. This collection of liturgies seeks to encourage the revival of an important Christian tradition of celebratory meals that has been largely forgotten today. This table fellow-ship has its religious roots in the Jewish tradition (cf. also the Dead Sea Qumran community) which still retains such meals and their associated prayers (such as in the Kiddush on Saturdays and the Seder at Passover, see nos **42** and **43** in this collection and the Glossary, p. 161). (For a simple and clear account of the Jewish background to the institution of the Eucharist, see Louis Bouyer, *Eucharist*, Paris, 1966 (London and University of Notre Dame, 1968), especially pp. 100–3).

Jesus lived in a world where eating and drinking with others had a significance we rarely appreciate today. The sharing of food and then a ritual drink was a common formula of a Graeco-Roman formal meal and had particular religious significance for Jews. Furthermore, Jesus introduced a new dimension to table fellowship. He practised a radical social egalitarianism that got him into trouble with his fellow Jews for being willing to eat and drink not just with friends but with anyone: heretics, unrepentant sinners, single women and social outcasts.

It has been suggested by some scholars (e.g. John Dominic Crossan, *The Historical Jesus: The Life of a Mediterranean Jewish Peasant*, T & T Clark, Edinburgh, 1991, pp. 360–7) that although there must logically have been one last meal which our Lord celebrated with his followers, the elements of Passover and the commemoration of his death were later developments of the Eucharist in the Christian community. The late first-century Syrian celebrations recorded in the Didache (see nos **15** and **16** in this collection) seem to attest to the existence of table celebrations without these elements which are today considered central to the Eucharist. In due course, it is suggested, Jesus' open table with real food, such as loaves and fishes, became a ritual meal confined to Christians. The desire to celebrate a meal in memory of Jesus, but with real food and open to everyone, has encouraged the revival of non-eucharistic (or pre-eucharistic) table liturgies in our own day.

In addition, we have tended to neglect those sharings of food and drink in our Lord's life which John Henson has called *Other Communions of Jesus* (Stantonbury Parish Print, 1994). Jesus produced a superior wine at a wedding, shared picnics with thousands at a time, drank water with a strange woman, and even made a point of picking his betrayer out for a special shared morsel as his life was inexorably drawing to its end. These other communions of Jesus can provide interesting models for table liturgies (see **Christ's Supper at Cana,** nos **19** and **20**).

But in Christianity, the Eucharist became the only shared meal. The agape fell into disuse, condemned in some of its aspects by St Paul, and forgotten after the eighth century. (An interesting eighteenth-century revival occurred with the Moravians and apparently survives today.)

But it is clear from the New Testament that another, rich, tradition has been lost. This includes that of the Chaburah, for example, the Jewish fellowship meal, making use of the familiar Jewish table blessings (Berakoth, see nos **10, 12** and **28** in this collection) but enriched by Jesus' creative usage. It is true that the Eucharist has also developed from these elements, but what has happened to this other tradition of table celebration? Hippolytus (antipope, martyr and saint) makes it plain in his writings that the two were distinct (*eucharistia* (Eucharist) and *eulogion* (Blessed Bread)), by the third century (see Dom Gregory Dix's *The Shape of the Liturgy*, 1945, p. 82).

Some hints of this alternative liturgical tradition still remain. In the Christian community, we often have grace before and after meals, celebratory parish banquets, informal coffee and chat or even blessed bread, after the service. Many monastic and other religious communities still celebrate their common meals with solemnity, involving a recollected atmosphere, prayers (sometimes extended and perhaps with psalms) and religious readings (see nos 9 and 11 in this collection). An interesting modern collection of graces before and after meals is that used at Our Lady of the Resurrection Monastery in LaGrangeville, New York (Victor-Antoine d'Avila-Latourrette, *Table Blessings*, Ave Maria Press, Notre Dame, Indiana, 1994).

It is time we returned to this early Christian tradition and brought the Agape back. We speak here not of house Eucharists presided over by ordained ministers and following substantially an order of service laid down by the authorities of the Church. We speak here of Christians celebrating meals together, using various forms, in an attempt to deepen their understanding of the gospel, the Eucharist, their baptismal priesthood, community and thus their own faith. With appropriate guidance and leadership, such celebrations can only assist Christians in their mission. There is clearly a place for *ecumenical* table celebrations of this type that fall short of breaching church order and which nevertheless reflect the imperfect communion already in existence.

In this alternative and ancient tradition, following a lead from Rome (Congregation for Divine Worship, *Book of Blessings*, 1984) the Catholic bishops of the United States in *Catholic Household Blessings and Prayers* (Bishops' Committee on the Liturgy, NCCB/USCC, Washington, 1988) propose a form of table blessing for use by families or house groups, with seasonal variations. The bishops' basic form is reproduced here as **13 At Table**. This collection contains many more liturgies, inspired by this revived tradition.

Agape or Eucharist?

Who can read the account of the feeding of the five thousand (John 6:5–15; and Matt. 14:13–21; Mark 6:32–44; Luke 9:10–17, and see no. 35 in this collection) where our Lord not only speaks of heavenly food, but also 'takes, blesses, breaks and shares' satisfying the crowd, without noting the same fourfold action in the Last Supper (Matt. 26:26; Mark 14:22; Luke 22:19)? Jesus clearly was adding something new to a ritual of meal blessings that was already familiar to his contemporaries, but largely lost to us, rather than inventing a new Church service.

Then we have the two accounts of Jesus revealing himself after his resurrection by this same action of taking, blessing, breaking and sharing food with his followers – in Luke's Gospel on the road to Emmaus (Luke 24:13–35, and see no. 33) and in John's Gospel on the beach (John 21, and see no. 31 in this collection). It is interesting that in John's account it is bread and fish that seem to be the central elements, contrasting with the bread and wine of our Eucharist and the Passover lamb of the Jews.

Scholars have argued that we have evidence from early Christian documents that our Lord made use of the Birkat-ha-Mazon (see the Glossary, p. 161). This collection therefore contains prayers based on this Jewish pattern (see nos 10, 12, 24 and 28).

A Table Liturgy can be defined as a meal, shared by Christians, often as a commemoration of one of the occasions where our Lord shared food or drink with others, and this definition would therefore also include the Eucharist. It is not clear if some of the earliest Christian celebrations of which we have the text and some account were Eucharists as well as agapes (see nos 15 and 16 from the *Didache*), and for this reason some of the liturgies in this book could in some circumstances perform both functions.

Those liturgies in this collection which contain the 'words of institution' are marked with an asterisk (*) in the Contents, as many Christians consider that their inclusion is essential for a Eucharist, although other conditions for canonical validity may also have to be met (such as a properly ordained president and an invocation of the Holy Spirit). On the other hand, the early anaphora of Addai and Mari does not explicitly contain the institution narrative but has not generally been considered 'invalid' (Jasper and Cuming, *Prayers of the Eucharist*, pp. 39–44 and Deiss, *Springtime of the Liturgy*, pp. 157–63).

In many cases the ambiguity may be healthy. Not everyone feels that the recitation of the institution narrative should always be reserved only to the lips of the formally ordained (see nos 27 and 28). Evidence suggests that in the first few centuries, lay women and men presided at the Eucharist, possibly representing continuity with Jewish table liturgies, where the head of the household would preside. Clerical control began for the sake of orderliness, it would seem, and eventually made itself indispensable.

The liturgies presented here are an attempt to encourage the growth and development of ecumenical Christian table fellowship, in the largely lost tradition of the Christian agape, as well as to lead to a deeper understanding and effective celebration of the Eucharist. By emulating our sisters and brothers the Jews, who still maintain an ancient tradition of table celebrations, we can share food and drink together in fellowship as Christians, calling to mind God's mighty works and making present once more his Son, since 'where two or three are gathered together, I am in their midst' (Matt. 18: 20).

Practical Points

It is important that nothing written here, or elsewhere, should be seen as other than suggestions as to how a good liturgy can be arranged. Readers must feel free to select, edit, adapt, omit and add as they wish. Some of the older liturgies in this collection do not use inclusive language, for example, and need to be amended. Of course, what may be suitable for husband and wife at home may not suit a larger family gathering. Sometimes just a grace before the meal is needed. At other times a group of friends may wish to have a table liturgy after a discussion and before a shared meal. We hope readers will experiment and create their own celebrations from the ideas presented in this book.

The section Other Resources (p. 173) lists books which will stimulate ideas. Two of these in particular deserve special mention and are mentioned below. In addition, the Worship Data Bank at 36 Court Lane, London SE21 7DR (tel: 0181-693 1438) has a resource bank of sheet liturgies and will offer advice on adapting worship to the needs of groups, families etc.

In 1988 the Bishops' Committee on the Liturgy of the United States National Conference of Catholic Bishops published its *Catholic Household Blessings & Prayers* (NCCB/USCC, Washington DC, 1988). It was an expansion and adaptation of the Vatican's *Book of Blessings* published in 1984. It contains blessings for numerous occasions, for particular days and seasons, for special occasions and family events, for various times and places. It has a most interesting section containing various table blessings. It enjoys, of course, full official approval.

Not enjoying such approval, but the fruit of the life and experience of the ecumenical Ashram Community Trust is *Community Worship Revised*, edited by John Vincent (Ashram Community Trust, Sheffield, 1987). This booklet makes a clear distinction between agapes and Eucharists, of which it contains several examples, and has a most useful practical introduction entitled 'Getting Worship Together' which covers much of the ground of this section.

Fuller celebrations, of the type this collection seeks to encourage, normally have four elements:

1. Readings with reflection and discussion;
2. Prayer in common, preferably with opportunities for individuals to make their own contributions;
3. A thanksgiving and commemoration of God's saving work, with perhaps specific mention of the redemptive work of Jesus Christ;
4. Sharing of food.

It is clearly important that everybody should be involved as much as is practical in such a celebration. When several hundred people are present in church, it is clearly impossible for the sense of individual participation to be as full as in a small house group celebration. This is one of the great advantages of a table liturgy in a small Christian community.

Preliminaries

Planning is essential. Although spontaneity is desirable, as one wishes to encourage people to make their own contributions, some structure is necessary to avoid embarrassment and uncertainty because of the unfamiliarity of the celebration to some of those present. It is important to avoid a rigidity of form, but if there is some structure present, some plan which the celebration is going to follow, then order is assured. This means that it is necessary to decide in advance who does what, in what order, what readings are to be chosen, how much time is to be given to each section, what food is to be eaten and who brings and prepares it.

It is important that everybody be as *actively involved* as possible. The leaders must therefore take care to obtain a consensus and make certain that all have a part to play. Not everyone may wish to say something in discussion, but a skilful Chair or host will make certain that people who are inclined to talk too much are discreetly and kindly discouraged and that signals are given for the next section to be moved to at the appropriate moment.

A third and similarly important factor is the scene chosen for the celebration and attention must be given to the *atmosphere* which is going to be generated. This is determined not only by the people who have chosen to attend but also by the venue, the food eaten and drunk, the order of events, size of the room, etc. It is important to strike a balance between formality and informality and between active and passive participants. In such celebrations there will inevitably be a number of newcomers as well as people who are already familiar with celebrations of this type. To a very great extent, of course, all must see themselves as taking part in a learning process and be open to new insights and new ways of seeing things.

Advance planning

A necessary requirement before a larger celebration of this kind can take place, and essentially bound up with its success, is the time and attention given to planning. The following items need to be thought about in advance:

1. The date and theme.
2. The time and place. Thought should also be given to the seating arrangements, what sort of comfort can be arranged, whether some people will be required to sit on the floor, whether people are to sit in rows or in a circle. It is not desirable for people to be looking at other people's backs, and a circle is the best arrangement if there is room.
3. Guests and hosts. How many newcomers are to be invited and what roles can one count on regular attenders playing?
4. Food and drink. It is usually preferable to decide on something simple, perhaps just bread and wine. What else is going to be eaten and drunk and who will bring it?
5. Order of events. It is better to plan too much than too little, as plans can always be abandoned or modified if the way things go suggests this. A common order of events might be:

> Introduction
> Readings
> Discussion
> Prayer
> Kiss of Peace
> Blessing of Food
> Meal

6. Key roles. Few are happy these days with one person dominating a celebration as president. Roles need to be assigned, so it is helpful if there is some sort of written or typed-out programme with various items numbered. The

assignation of roles can be done at the last minute or it can just be agreed that each person round the room takes it in turn to recite the next numbered item on the sheet, taking care to perform any actions specified (e.g. 'taking some bread'). Alternatively, the group can be divided into two, taking the odd and even numbered items alternately. It is important that the Chair or host be absolutely clear as to what is planned so as to avoid confusion, and should have a written note of which person is doing what. It is often worthwhile deciding on some sort of music, sung solo or together, or even played from a cassette or CD.

Introduction

Someone needs to introduce the celebration, to explain what is expected of participants and what form the readings and discussion will take. It may also be appropriate for participants to introduce themselves in turn. Some form of act of penance or opening prayer may also be appropriate and needs to be prepared for (see especially nos 2 to 8).

Readings

A celebration of this type is a marvellous opportunity to depart from the normal ecclesiastical practice of restricting oneself to readings from Scripture. Alan Dale's *Winding Quest* and *New World* (Oxford University Press, 1972 and 1967) are excellent modern paraphrases of the Bible, which by their very freshness prove illuminating when read to those long familiar with traditional translations. Devotional or theological works are also sources of fruitful material and different groups and individuals will be able to make various proposals. St Philip Neri in the sixteenth century had readings from the letters of missionaries and extracts from reports read at his celebrations. Today we have videos, cassettes and CDs available to us. Topical extracts from newspapers and other publications can often prove very stimulating and thought-provoking too.

Discussion

If at all possible, it is desirable that there be some discussion of an informal kind about the readings or the topics chosen. It is helpful to arrange for some people to begin the discussion by having given some thought in advance to what they might say, and others can be primed to make strategic points or to formulate questions in order to encourage others to participate. Essential is an unobtrusive Chair, able to generate discussion and to assist the diffident to make their voices heard. When people are brought to share their faith, their hesitations, their doubts, their hopes and their prayers with others, this always proves a strengthening and supportive experience for all involved. It is the Spirit working.

Prayer

Celebrations of this type are an excellent opportunity for people to use extempore prayer. It is important however that biddings end with some sort of signal for a response. Thus, each petition could end with 'Lord (or God) in your mercy', to which all are then able to respond without hesitation in one voice 'Hear our prayer'. More familiar to some are the forms 'Lord hear us' with its response 'Lord, graciously hear us'. It does not matter, of course, if different forms are used by different people. Thought might also be given as to whether a suitable collect or prayer from the Church's liturgy might not have a place, and whether the Our Father might not also be appropriate at some point.

It is important also to give consideration to the place of silence. This can be awkward if participants are not used to it, but groups that meet regularly have found that they welcome periods when they can reflect on what has been read or said or done, and can pray in their own hearts. Decisions need to be made in advance how long such periods of silence should be, and how they are to be ended, by what signal and by whom.

Equally important for many is music. Here again, some groups that meet regularly enjoy singing together and can do so without embarrassment. A keyboard or guitar, or indeed other instruments can find a place, but are not essential. Sometimes there are suitable recordings or extracts from videos that can find a place in a celebration and prove very moving.

The Peace

Most Christians are familiar with the Kiss of Peace in church, and it is often appropriate to include this in the celebration at some point. The most ancient position for this liturgically is before the table blessing. For some people a real kiss is often more appropriate than a handshake or a hug.

Blessing of the Food and Drink

The items in the present collection range from very simple forms to much more complex blessings. There is surely no need to ask questions about 'validity'. In a celebration meal of this type, we are concerned only with having an effective celebration. We may not all necessarily intend to re-create the Eucharist, and indeed it is sometimes not possible to be clear about the objectives of everyone present. We do not ask whether a birthday party or a wedding reception is 'valid'. We only ask ourselves, 'What has this celebration set out to do, and has it successfully achieved its aims?'

This collection contains some very simple short blessings (such as nos 17, 23 and 24) as well as some longer forms, some with the Institution Narrative and some without. Not all participants may be ready to use what they consider 'the words of consecration', so some care needs to be taken in selecting a form appropriate to those who will be present. (The liturgies in this book which contain the words of institution are marked *. In fact, liturgical scholars point out that these words have not always appeared in every form of the Eucharist. Their recitation outside a Church Eucharist may however cause difficulties for some and should obviously be avoided if offence might be caused.)

A decision may need to be taken whether food and drink are to be consumed when taken from the table or whether all are to wait and consume collectively.

Meal

It is important that any meal is as fully integrated as possible with the table liturgy and that awkwardness is avoided. Sometimes a clear break is desirable after what has preceded, before the company can be expected to begin eating and drinking. This break can become an embarrassment if it is not carefully planned. A good solution is to make certain that the food is already present in the room before the celebration begins, or is at least capable of being brought in within thirty seconds or so. One could

perhaps arrange for certain people taking part in the celebration to continue the discussion while a couple of others
unobtrusively bring in the meal, so that the blessing can
follow and the meal immediately after it.

Alternatives to Familiar Texts

Opening
✝ In the name of God, the Creator, and of Jesus the Redeemer
and of the Holy Spirit. Amen.

Glory be
Glory be to God our Creator
to Jesus the Christ,
and to the Holy Spirit who dwells in our midst,
both now and for ever. Amen.

Glory to you
Glory to you, Source of all Being,
Eternal Word, and Holy Spirit;

As it was in the beginning,
is now and ever shall be,
world without end. Amen.

The Pattern Prayers, GEMS Reset,
ONE for Christian Renewal

Our Father
Loving God, here and everywhere,
help us to proclaim your values
and bring in your New World.
Supply us with our day-to-day needs.
Forgive us for wounding you,

while we forgive those who wound us.
Give us courage to meet life's trials
and deal with evil's power.
We celebrate your New World,
full of life and beauty,
lasting for ever. Amen.

The Pattern Prayers, GEMS Reset,
ONE for Christian Renewal

Preparatory and Penitential Liturgies

Prophecies

This liturgy is a series of prophecies of the New Covenant from the Hebrew Bible. They raise the questions to what extent these prophecies are already fulfilled and what we are still waiting for. Discussion and prayer can follow and then a table liturgy.

1   Let us say together:

ALL   **Blessed are you, Lord, God of all creation, for your promises to us through your prophet Jeremiah:**

2   See, the days are coming – it is the Lord who speaks – when I will make a new covenant with the House of Israel and the House of Judah, but not a covenant like the one I made with your ancestors on the day I took them by the hand to bring them out of the land of Egypt.

3   They broke that covenant of mine, so I had to show them who was master. It is the Lord who speaks. No, this is the covenant I will make with the House of Israel when those days arrive – it is the Lord who speaks.

4   Deep within them I will plant my Law, writing it on their hearts. Then I will be their God and they shall be my people. There will be no further need for neighbour to try to teach neighbour, or one to say to another, 'Learn to know the Lord!'

5   No, they will all know me, the least no less than the
     greatest – it is the Lord who speaks – since I will
     forgive their iniquity and never call their sin to
     mind.

                                              (Jer. 31:31–4, JB)

6   Let us say together:

**ALL   Blessed are you, Lord, God of all creation,
         for your promises to us through your prophet
         Hosea:**

7   When that day comes I will make a treaty on her
     behalf with the wild animals, with the birds of
     heaven and the creeping things of the earth; I will
     break bow, sword and battle in the country, and
     make her sleep secure.

8   I will betroth you to myself for ever, betroth you
     with integrity and justice, with tenderness and love;
     I will betroth you to myself with faithfulness, and
     you will come to know the Lord.

                                              (Hos. 2:20–2, JB)

9   Let us say together:

**ALL   Blessed are you, Lord, God of all creation,
         for your promises to us through your prophet
         Ezekiel:**

10   The Lord God says this: I am not doing this for your
     sake, House of Israel, but for the sake of my holy
     name, which you have profaned among the nations
     where you have gone. I mean to display the holiness
     of my great name, which has been profaned among

                              5

the nations, which you have profaned among them.
And the nations will learn that I am the Lord – it is
the Lord God who speaks – when I display my
holiness for your sake before their eyes.

11 Then I am going to take you from among the
nations and gather you together from all the foreign
countries, and bring you home to your own land. I
shall pour clean water over you and you shall be
cleansed; I shall cleanse you of all your defilement
and all your idols. I shall give you a new heart and
put a new spirit in you. I shall remove the heart of
stone from your bodies and give you a heart of flesh
instead. I shall put my spirit in you, and make you
keep my laws and sincerely respect my observances.

(Ezek. 36:22–8, JB)

12 Let us say together:

ALL **Blessed are you, Lord, God of all creation,
for your promises to us through your prophet
Isaiah:**

13 With you I will make an everlasting covenant out of
the favours promised to David. See, I have made of
you a witness to the peoples, a leader and a master
of the nations. See, you will summon a nation you
never knew, those unknown will come hurrying to
you, for the sake of the Lord your God, of the Holy
One of Israel who will glorify you.

(Isa. 55:3–5, JB)

*Further readings (Isaiah 61:1–9 and Romans 8:14–39 are
especially recommended), discussion and prayer, now
follow.*

A Preparation

*This is a prayer of preparation which can be used before any table liturgy (especially **34** for which it was written), perhaps with a liturgy of penance immediately following it, such as **3**, **Form A**.*

1 We are about to re-enact
   the great event
   that gives meaning to our lives,
   so let us put ourselves in a suitable frame of mind.

2 This celebration is one of thanksgiving,
   or gratitude,
   for the ability to overcome evil.

3 To appreciate this fully,
   let us make ourselves open to the chaos,
   evil and futility in our lives.

4 To see the task we have set ourselves,
   let us acknowledge,
   in a few moments of silence,
   the evil that we
   and our way of life
   inflict on the whole world.

3   Two Acts of Penance

Two short acts of penance, to be used before other liturgies.

Form A

ALL   We stand here before God
        and all the people of God,
        acknowledging our failure
        to follow the way of Christ
        in our lives.

        We ask your forgiveness.

        We ask you Father
        to give us the light to see,
        and the courage to carry out,
        your will.

        We ask for the help of your Holy Spirit
        in the carrying out of this resolve
        for all the people of God,
        especially those here present.

Form B

1   Let us in silence remember our own faults and failings.

A period of reflection follows.

2   If we say we are without sin,
        we are blind and will not see.

3   If we say our world is all right,
    we are deaf and will not hear.

4   Let us therefore acknowledge our sin,
    and stand as people who are forgiven
    and free to serve.

ALL   **Merciful God,**
      we confess that we have sinned,
      in thought, word and deed,
      we have not loved you with all our heart.
      We have not loved our neighbour as ourselves.

      In your mercy, forgive what we have been,
      help us to change what we are,
      and direct what we shall be;
      that we may do justly,
      love mercifully,
      and walk humbly with you. Amen.

4   Preparation and Kyrie

*A form of penance and reconciliation, written round
the threefold Kyrie, and ending with the kiss of peace.*

1   Let us rejoice that we are gathered here to
     celebrate ...

The celebration and its theme are now introduced.

2   Let us join in saying together:

**ALL   We have come to this day through darkness
         and through moments of light,
         along paths of pain.
         Always we have travelled with the hope
         that lies in the shared human journey.**

3   Let us prepare ourselves for this celebration
     by calling to mind our faults and failings.

A time for reflection follows. Then:

4   O God, you created us in your image.

**ALL   For all the times we have not believed this,
         Lord, have mercy.**

5   You breathed the breath of life into us.

**ALL   For all the times when we have chosen
         not to affirm that life,
         Christ, have mercy.**

6   You redeemed us from sin.

ALL   **For all the times when we have turned away from you,**
Lord, have mercy.

Spirit of God,
we believe you have redeemed us.
Forgive us our faults and failings.
Help us to live and work
towards wholeness and holiness.

7   Let us share peace as a sign of reconciliation with each other, the world, and ourselves.

A sign of peace is exchanged.

Liturgy of Penance for Sins of Divisiveness

A liturgy that brings us to face our destructive failings and unites us in a commitment to service and ministry.

Reading: Genesis 4:2(b)–8

Litany:

1   If we have been envious,

℞   **Forgive us Lord!**

2   If we have set ourselves apart from others by scorning them,

℞   **Forgive us Lord!**

3   If we have failed to try to see things from the point of view of another – a husband, a wife, a child, a colleague,

℞   **Forgive us Lord!**

4   If we have damaged a human community by being deceitful or unreliable,

℞   **Forgive us Lord!**

5   If we have cherished our grudges after they should have been buried,

℞   **Forgive us Lord!**

6   If we have neglected opportunities for making
     peace,

℟   **Forgive us Lord!**

7   If we have been sulky and withdrawn our love,

℟   **Forgive us Lord!**

8   If we have provoked others
     by probing their known weaknesses,

℟   **Forgive us Lord!**

9   If we have tried to impose our view on others
     against their will,

℟   **Forgive us Lord!**

10   If we have closed our eyes
     to avoid seeing the needs of others,

℟   **Forgive us Lord!**

11   If we are content to see the followers of Christ
     divided into separate communions,

℟   Forgive us Lord!

12   If we have given tacit support through our govern-
     ment
     to grave injustices and all the suffering entailed,

℟   **Forgive us Lord!**

13   If we have shrugged off responsibility
     for the casualties in the life of the nation,

℟   **Forgive us Lord!**

14   If we have decided
that our own European standard of living must be
defended
even if it means that half the world's people
go under-nourished,

℞   **Forgive us Lord!**

15   If we have aided and abetted oppression,
exploitation, discrimination or any unjust violence,

℞   **Forgive us Lord!**

16   If we have forgotten that our baptism is a call to a
life of service and ministry,

℞   **Forgive us Lord!**

ALL   **Father,
break the cycle of evil that holds us captive.
Let sin die in us,
as the sin of the world died in Jesus, your Son.
In him, death too was killed.
He lives again,
for you
and for us,
here and now,
today and every day.
Amen.**

Come, Lord Jesus!

Short Liturgy of Reconciliation 6

*A liturgy that makes us face up to the call of the gospel
and our refusal to listen and act.*

Readings

Psalm 32

Micah 7:8–20

Matthew 9

Examination of Conscience

1   Do we readily forgive each other,
or do we harbour wounds and hate within our
hearts?

2   Do we seek out the poor and the oppressed,
endeavouring to help them in their struggle for
dignity,
or do we put them in our litanies of prayer
and refuse to act?

3   Do we put ourselves with Jesus
on the side of people in need,
or do we allow ourselves to be paralysed by fear
or the temptations of wealth
and forget what we would rather not know?

ALL   I am listening to what the Lord God is saying.
He promises peace to us his own people,
if we do not go back to our foolish ways.

4   Are we willing to answer God's call to be disciples,
     to be bearers of the good news,
     or do we cling to our security
     and proclaim our poverty of spirit?

5   Do we work for justice for oppressed people
     or do we prefer to think of them as lazy and stupid?

6   Do we seek the crucified Christ in the poor
     and speak out with the prophet's tongue,
     or do we prefer to limit our view
     and speak quietly in platitudes?

ALL **I am listening to what the Lord God is saying.**
     He promises peace to us his own people,
     if we do not go back to our foolish ways.

7   Do we accept our responsibility to be peace-makers,
     or do we passively allow aggression
     to be part of our lives?

8   Are we willing to risk building a just peace
     rather than arming ourselves for war?

9   Are we willing to accept the rule of the Prince of
     Peace
     and the power of the resurrection,
     or do we prefer to shut our doors
     to the pains of the poor
     and pretend they are not there?

ALL **I am listening to what the Lord God is saying.**
     He promises peace to us his own people,
     if we do not go back to our foolish ways.

Preparatory and Penitential Liturgies

Confession

ALL   Creator God,
you have called us to serve the cause of right;
you have chosen us to bring true justice to the nations
and to be messengers of your freedom
to those who are not treated as your children.

We confess together our failures in your service
and ask forgiveness and healing,
for we are not worthy;
but your love makes us your children.

Have mercy on us,
as we make our prayer through your son,
our Lord, Jesus Christ.

Absolution

ALL   May almighty God have mercy on us his children.
May he forgive us,
as a loving parent forgives a contrite child.
May he bless us with new hope
and a determination to live according to his word,
our Lord Jesus Christ. Amen.

19

7   Liturgy of Hope

A liturgy that seeks to listen to the Spirit and examine our failure to respond in true Christian witness to the modern world.

A candle is lit and the following said:

1   May the power and mystery go before us
to show us the way,
shine above us to lighten our world,
lie beneath us to bear us up,
walk with us and give us companionship,
and glow and flow within us to bring us joy.

From Psalm 17

ALL   Loving Creator, hear our prayer
and listen to our call made in the spirit of truth.

You know what we are,
and that we seek to be faithful to you.
We search your word to find our way.
Let us walk in your footsteps
so that our feet do not slip.

We call on you, O Creator of life
and you answer us.
Listen to our voice
and show us your loving kindness,
O saviour of all who flee from evil.

Strengthen us in the struggle to do your will,
let our reward be to see you face to face,
and come into your loving presence.

Penitential prayer

Two groups might most effectively take it in turns to say the odd numbered and the even numbered sections that follow in this prayer, or each can be said by one person in turn.

1   Loving Creator,
who has breathed your own life into your people,
you have given us all creation to care for,
the tall trees of the forest and the crops of the fields,
the fish that swim in the sea
and the animals that roam the earth:
all the good things that you made.

2   And we, what have we done with your gifts?
We have used the resources of the earth recklessly,
plundered the riches of this planet with greed
and refused to share with the poor and the hungry.

ALL   Forgive us, O Source of all our being,
and bring us back into harmony with your universe.

3   We are called to love one another in your name,
yet what have we done?
We talk about love with our lips –

4   But we pass on the other side
when needs press in upon us.
Rules matter more than compassion,
the law than the spirit.

ALL   **Forgive us for our failure to listen to your call
to show forth your love in our lives
and that of the Church.**

5   We have been called to be sisters and brothers of Christ,
yet what have we done?
We have allowed the dominations
and oppressions of the world
to enter into Christ's body.

6   We have failed to listen to each other
although we are all called
to be a chosen race, a royal priesthood
and a consecrated nation.

ALL   **Send forth your Spirit into our hearts
so that we may truly share with one another
the work of building up your realm
here on earth.**

7   You created human beings in your own image;
'male and female, God created them.'

8   Yet your people have treated women,
made in the image of God,
as inferior and defective.

ALL   **Help us to build up a true community
of women and men in the Church,
where sexual and racial discrimination is overcome.**

9   God our liberator,
through Christ's redeeming act we have been made free
and brought out into the light.

10   Yet we fear to act as prophets
     when we see that things need changing.

ALL   **Forgive us, O loving Creator,
      for our lack of courage.
      Send forth your Spirit
      and make your new creation truly effective in us.
      Help all your people
      to work together in love and trust
      to build up the body of Christ.**

8

Liturgy of Good News

A prayer that we might recognize the presence of God and bring about the new life promised by Jesus Christ.

1   O God, Creator, Redeemer and Sustainer,
Pattern of mutual love,
forgive us for failing to understand
that being Church means loving well.

℟   **Help us to create loving community.**

2   God of justice and integrity, forgive us
for all the times we have not identified ourselves
with the oppressed and deprived,
and for the times we have put down others.

℟   **Help us to uphold each other.**

3   God the disturber, forgive us
for the times we have taken the easy path in comfort
rather than facing discomfort in spreading your
good news.

℟   **Help us to be joyful announcers of the word.**

4   God, maker of both men and women in your own
image
forgive us for presenting a distorted understanding
of what it means to be human or divine.

℟   **Help us to mirror the truth.**

5   O Creator God, forgive us
     for not affirming the goodness
     of the bodies you have given us,
     and for forgetting the importance of Mary
     caressing Jesus' feet with her hair.

℟   **Help us to accept ourselves
     in our God-given wholeness.**

6   O God, friend and lover, forgive us
     for our failing to understand our calling
     to friendship and honesty.

℟   **Help us to be creative and healing
     in our relationships.**

7   O God, source of all insight,
     forgive us our shallow understanding of your pres-
     ence,
     when we fail to recognize the meal taken together,
     the joy or sorrow shared,
     as a meeting with the divine.
     Strengthen our understanding
     so that our lives may become more Christlike
     and so draw others to you.

℟   **Help us to recognize
     where you are among us.**

ALL **O Spirit that empowers the powerless,
     give us the strength
     to forge communities of loving friends
     to bring about the new life
     promised in the resurrection.**

Table Blessings

From the Psalter

9

A grace before meals based on that used in many Benedictine monasteries.

1   *Someone says:*

The eyes of all hope in you, Lord,

℟   **And you give them food in due season.**

2   *Someone else, or the leader, says:*

You open your hand,

℟   **And every creature is filled with your blessings.**

3   *A third person, or the leader, says:*

Blessed is God in his gifts,

℟   **And holy in all his works.**

The Jewish Blessings

A grace before meals based on the traditional Jewish blessings.

1   *Holding a piece of bread for all to see:*

Blessed are you, Lord, God of all creation
for you bring forth bread from the earth.

*The bread is broken and passed round, or the whole piece
is passed for each to break some off.*

2   *Taking a cup of wine and holding it up:*

Blessed are you, Lord, God of all creation,
creator of the fruit of the vine.

The wine is passed round for all to drink.

A Community Grace

A form of grace for before and after meals which was used by the Anglican monks of Nashdom Abbey.

Before eating:

   1   In the name of the Father
          and of the Son
          and of the Holy Spirit.

℟   **Amen.**

   2   Blessed be God, the Creator of all things.

℟   **Thanks be to God, who has given us life and all that sustains it.**

   3   Let us pray for all those through whom our food is provided.

℟   **Bless them O Lord.**

After eating:

   1   Let us who have shared in this meal pray for each other.

℟   **May God unite us in heart and in his service.**

   2   Let us pray for all who are in hunger or need.

℟   **Bless them O Lord.**

3 May the Lord who has fed us on earth
   bring us to share his banquet in heaven.

℞ **Amen.**

12

*A Table Blessing

A simple grace before meals that is based on the form known by Jesus and his disciples. It includes the words which Jesus added at the Last Supper.

1   *Someone takes some bread and holding it up over the food that has been brought for sharing says:*

Blessed are you, Lord, God of all creation. You nourish the whole world with goodness, tender love and mercy. Through your goodness we have this food, which earth has given and human hands have made. Jesus said 'This is my body!' May it become for us the bread of life.

℞   **Blessed be God for ever!**

The bread is broken and passed round.

2   *Someone else takes some wine and holding it up over the food which has been brought for sharing says:*

Blessed are you, Lord, God of all creation. You have made us a royal priesthood, a consecrated people. Through your goodness we have this drink, the fruit of the vine and the work of human hands. Jesus said 'This is my blood!' May it become our spiritual drink.

℞   **Blessed be God for ever!**

The wine is passed round.

3   *A third person says:*

Blessed are you, Lord, God of all creation. We remember with gratitude our redemption and wait in joyful hope for the coming of our Saviour, Jesus Christ.

℞   **For the kingdom, the power and the glory are yours, now and for ever!**

4   *Another person says:*

Let us proclaim the mystery of faith.

ALL   **When we eat this bread and drink this cup, we proclaim your death, Lord Jesus, until you come in glory!**

13

At Table

A form of grace before meals proposed by the bishops of the Catholic Church in the USA.

When all are seated, begin with the sign of the cross:

> **In the name of the Father,†**
> **and of the Son,**
> **and of the Holy Spirit. Amen.**

1   Lord, the lover of life,
    you feed the birds of the skies
    and array the lilies of the field.
    We bless you for all your creatures
    and for the food we are about to receive.
    We humbly pray that in your goodness
    you will provide for our brothers and sisters
    who are hungry.
    We ask this through Christ our Lord.

ALL   **Amen.**

2   Blessed are you, almighty Father,
    who gives us our daily bread.
    Blessed is your only begotten Son,
    who continually feeds us
    on the word of life.
    Blessed is the Holy Spirit,
    who brings us together at this table of love.
    Blessed be God, now and for ever.

ALL   **Amen.**

Table Blessings

Bread may be lifted up and broken:

3   Blessed are you, Lord, God of all creation:
you bring forth bread from the earth.
Blessed be God for ever.

℟   **Blessed be God for ever.**

A cup of wine may be lifted up.

4   Blessed are you, Lord, God of all creation:
creator of the fruit of the vine.
Blessed be God for ever.

℟   **Blessed be God for ever.**

5   Let us call on the name of the Father,
who always takes care of his children.

℟   **Our Father …**
For the kingdom, the power, and the glory are yours,
now and for ever.

6   Lord, our God,
with fatherly love you come to the aid of your
children.
Bless us and these † your gifts
which we are about to receive from your goodness.
Grant that all peoples may be gladdened
by the favours of your providence.
We ask this through Christ our Lord.

℟   **Amen.**

or the following prayer may be said:

6   God of all goodness,
through the breaking of bread together
you strengthen the bonds that unite us in love.
Bless ✝ us and these your gifts.
Grant that as we sit down together at table
in joy and sincerity,
we may grow always closer in the bonds of love.
We ask this through Christ our Lord.

℟   **Amen.**

7   May your gifts refresh us, O Lord,
and your grace give us strength.

℟   **Amen.**

A New Covenant Liturgy

14

A celebration of the priesthood of all the baptized, followed by the previous grace (13), that can precede a celebratory meal.

ALL   **In the name of the Father,
and of the Son,
and of the Holy Spirit. Amen.**

1   Blessed are you, Lord God of all creation, for your promises to us through your prophet Isaiah:

Come here to me and hear what I have to say
and learn the secret of really being alive:
I will make an unbreakable covenant with you,
and give you my steadfast love
as I gave it to King David!
I made *him* a witness to the world, a leader and a commander;
so shall *you* hail nations you have never heard of.
They shall come running to you –
for God, the Holy One of his people,
has shone in glory upon *you*!

Blessed be God for ever!

℟   **Blessed be God for ever.**

2   Blessed are you, Lord God of all creation, for your
      promises to us through your prophet Jeremiah:

      This is the new covenant I will make with the whole
      people:
      My Way shall be clear to everybody's conscience,
      something everyone can recognize;
      I will *really* be their God,
      and they shall *really* be *My People*.

      Blessed be God for ever!

℟   **Blessed be God for ever.**

3   Blessed are you, Lord God of all creation, for your
      promises to us through your prophet Hosea:

      I will betroth you to myself for ever,
      betroth you with integrity and justice,
      with tenderness and love.
      I will betroth you to myself with faithfulness,
      and you will come to *know* the Lord.

      Blessed be God for ever!

℟   **Blessed be God for ever.**

4   Blessed are you, Lord God of all creation, for your
      promises to us through your prophet Ezekiel:

      The Lord God says this: I shall give you a new heart,
      and put a new spirit in you.
      I shall remove the heart of stone from your bodies
      and give you a heart of flesh instead.
      I shall put my Spirit in you and make you keep my
      laws and sincerely respect my observances.
      You shall be *My People* –
      and I shall be your God.

Blessed be God for ever!

℞   **Blessed be God for ever.**

5   Blessed are you, Lord God of all creation, for your
promises to us through your prophet Joel:

I will pour out my Spirit on *all humankind*.
Your sons and daughters shall prophesy;
your old men shall dream dreams,
and your young men see visions.
Even on the slaves, men and women,
will I pour out my Spirit in those days.

Blessed be God for ever!

℞   **Blessed be God for ever.**

6   Blessed are you, Lord God of all creation, for your
promises to us through your Son, Jesus Christ:

If people love me, they will keep my word,
and my Father will love them,
and we shall come to them
and make our *home* with them.

This is the gospel of the Lord!

℞   **Praise to you, Lord Jesus Christ!**

The blessing of the food now follows:

7   Lord, the lover of life,
you feed the birds of the skies
and array the lilies of the field.
We bless you for all your creatures
and for the food we are about to receive.
We humbly pray that in your goodness

you will provide for our brothers and sisters
who are hungry.
We ask this through Christ our Lord.

ALL   **Amen.**

8   Blessed are you, almighty Father,
who gives us our daily bread.
Blessed is your only begotten Son,
who continually feeds us
on the word of life.
Blessed is the Holy Spirit,
who brings us together at this table of love.
Blessed be God for ever.

℟   **Blessed be God for ever.**

Bread is lifted up and broken:

9   Blessed are you, Lord, God of all creation:
you bring forth bread from the earth.
Blessed be God for ever.

℟   **Blessed be God for ever.**

A cup of wine is lifted up.

10   Blessed are you, Lord, God of all creation:
creator of the fruit of the vine.
Blessed be God for ever.

℟   **Blessed be God for ever.**

11   Let us call on the name of the Father,
who always takes care of his children.

℟   **Our Father …**
For the kingdom, the power, and the glory are yours,
now and for ever.

12   God of all goodness,
through the breaking of bread together
you strengthen the bonds that unite us in love.
Bless ✝ us and these your gifts.
Grant that as we sit down together at table
in joy and sincerity,
we may grow always closer in the bonds of love.
We ask this through Christ our Lord.

℞   **Amen.**

13   May your gifts refresh us, O Lord, and your grace give us strength.

℞   **Amen.**

15   An Early Table Thanksgiving
from the *Didache*

A reconstruction from a very early Christian table liturgy which can be used as grace after a meal.

1   We give you thanks, Father, for your holy name, which you have caused to live in our hearts, and for the knowledge and faith and everlasting life which you have revealed to us through your Servant Jesus.

℟   **Glory to you for ever!**

2   You created everything, almighty Lord, for your name's sake. You have given food and drink to everyone for them to enjoy, that they might give you thanks. But to us you have graciously given spiritual food and drink and everlasting life through your Servant Jesus. Above all, we thank you because you are almighty.

℟   **Glory to you for ever!**

3   Lord, remember your Church; deliver it from all evil; perfect it in your love; gather it, sanctified, from the four winds into the kingdom you have prepared for it.

℟   **For the kingdom, the power and the glory are yours, now and for ever! Amen.**

4   Let grace come and let this world pass away.

℟   **Hosanna to the God of David!**

16   A Later Table Thanksgiving
From the *Didache*

A reconstruction from a very early Christian table blessing, pre-Eucharistic, especially suitable for a group where a shared Eucharist would be inappropriate. It is also a popular grace before meals.

1   *Taking some wine and pouring some into each glass:*

We give you thanks, Father, for the vine of your servant David, which you have made known to us through your Servant Jesus.

℟   **Glory to you for ever!**

2   *Taking some bread:*

We give you thanks, Father, for the life and knowledge you have revealed to us through your Servant Jesus.

℟   **Glory to you for ever!**

3   *Breaking the bread and passing it round:*

Just as this broken bread, once scattered over the hills, was brought together and became one loaf, so may your Church be brought together from the ends of the earth into your kingdom.

℟   **For the kingdom, the power and the glory are yours, now and for ever! Amen.**

Thanksgiving Meal Prayer 17

A grace suitable for use before a celebratory meal.

1   *Taking some bread and holding it up over the food that has been brought for sharing:*

We give you thanks, Creator of the universe. You give us every good gift. Through your goodness we have life and breath. We share this bread as a sign of your steadfast love and care. We bless and thank you today.

℞   **Blessed be God for ever!**

The bread is broken and passed round, but NOT EATEN yet.

2   *A second person says:*

Just as this bread was once scattered grains across the hills and brought together to form one loaf, so may your Church be brought together from the ends of the earth into your kingdom.

℞   **Blessed be God for ever!**

The bread is now eaten.

3   *A third person says:*

May this bread and all the food we share at this meal nourish us and keep us mindful of our oneness in the Lord, so that we may bring about the kingdom of God, in our hearts and in the world.

℞   **Blessed be God for ever!**

18

An Agape

An agape celebrating the unity of humankind, suitable for all believers in God, not just Christians.

1   We believe that all people are the children of God,
    and therefore have worth and dignity.

2   All are welcome to share in this agape meal,
    without regard for human divisions of race, sexuality, class or creed.

3   As we prepare to follow the example of Jesus in sharing this bread and wine,
    let us affirm our faith.

4   Sisters and brothers,
    let us dedicate ourselves anew
    to live in such a way that justice may roll like waters,
    that peace may become real,
    that the dignity of all persons may be manifest.

5   Let us make a covenant with one another
    and seek to make a new beginning.

6   Let us declare solemnly
    that we are at peace with all people of good will.

℞   **We seek peace with all people.**

7   We affirm that our security rests not in armaments.
    We seek a just economic order
    in which everyone has access to the abundance of the earth.

We seek justice in human relationships,
nourished in the solidarity of the human family.

℟   **We affirm justice for all people.**

8   We choose struggle rather than indifference.
We choose to be friends of the earth and of one
another,
not exploiters.
We choose to be citizens rather than subjects.
We choose to be peace-makers rather than peace-
keepers.

℟   **We choose life for all creation.**

9   We join with sisters and brothers the world over.
We join in communities of resistance
to the threat of hunger and injustice,
to the threat of nuclear destruction.

℟   **We unite to resist the powers of death.**

10   Before us today are set life and death.

℟   **We choose life that we and our children may live.**

All share the bread and wine.

19

Christ's Supper at Cana I

A liturgy celebrating Jesus Christ, the new wine, appropriate where a newly married couple are present.

Bread or wedding cake, water and wine are put out.

1   Jesus' mother was a guest at a wedding in the village of Cana in Galilee, and Jesus and his disciples were invited too. Jesus is *here*!

℞   **His spirit is with us.**

2   The bridegroom has come!

℞   **Let the festivities begin!**

3   He brings his peace.

℞   **Let us share it with one another.**

A sign of peace is shared.

4   *Taking the bread or cake, someone says:*

Let us ask God's blessing.

℞   **God, bless these gifts to our delight,**
     and ourselves to be your friends,
     in the name of Jesus Christ. Amen.

The bread or cake is broken and handed round for eating.
Then someone says:

5   The wine supply ran out during the festivities, and Jesus' mother came to him with the problem. She told the servants, 'Do whatever he tells you.' Six stone waterpots were standing there. Jesus told the servant to fill them to the brim with water. When this was done, he said, 'Dip some out and take it to the master of ceremonies.'

A cup of water is passed round.

6   When the master of ceremonies tasted the water that was now wine, he called the bridegroom over. 'This is wonderful stuff!' he said. 'You're different from most. Usually a host uses the best wine first, but you have kept the best wine till last!'

Wine is passed round.

7   Whenever we eat or drink together

℟   **We are in the company of Jesus,
our friend and life-giver.**

20   Christ's Supper at Cana II

A liturgy recalling Jesus' call to be joyful, to eat and drink with him, to celebrate!

Bread, water and wine are put out.

1   Eat your bread with enjoyment
and drink your wine in happiness,
because God favours your work.

2   God of joy and high spirits!

3   God of laughter and fun!

4   We accept your invitation to eat and drink with you.

5   We come to enjoy the life you offer us in Jesus.

6   May our joy be rooted in your love.

ALL   **In God's name. Amen.**

7   Jesus, we pray for those who seem not to have joy.
(Names may be mentioned here.)

8   Let them hear through us your invitation
to the community of love and peace.

9   Whenever we eat and drink together,
we are in the company of Jesus,
our friend and life-giver.

ALL   Loving God, help us to proclaim your values.
Supply us with our day-to-day needs.
Forgive us for rejecting you,
while we forgive those who wound us.
Give us courage to meet life's trials
and deal with evil's power.
We celebrate your kingdom,
full of life and beauty,
lasting for ever. Amen.

10   Jesus' mother, and Jesus and his disciples, were invited to a wedding.

ALL   His spirit is with us too.

Someone takes some bread and all say:

ALL   God, bless these gifts to our joy,
and ourselves to be your friends.

Bread is broken and handed round for eating. Then someone says:

11   The wine supply ran out during the festivities, and Jesus' mother took the problem to him. She said to the servants, 'Do what he says.'

12   Jesus told them to fill the waterpots. When this was done he said, 'Take a cup of this to the master of ceremonies.'

13   When the master of ceremonies tasted the water that was now wine, he said to the bridegroom, 'You have kept the best wine to the end!'

14   Let us ask God's blessing.

ALL   **God, bless this wine to our joy,
and ourselves to be your friends.**

Wine is passed round.

15   Whenever

ALL   **we eat and drink together,
we are in the company of Jesus, our life-giver.**

16   We pray for your pilgrim Church,
that she may experience and radiate your love
throughout the universe.
Let us be at peace.

ALL   **Amen!**

An extended liturgy of recommitment which takes place round a meal, suitable for a group of Christian friends who are used to praying and working together.

Introduction

1   *Someone places a lighted candle on the table and says:*

Jesus Christ, the Light of the World.

ALL   **Our Father in heaven,**
hallowed be your name;
your kingdom come;
your will be done
on earth as in heaven.
Give us today our daily bread.
Forgive us our sins,
as we forgive those who sin against us.
Do not bring us to the time of trial,
but deliver us from evil.
For the kingdom, the power, and the glory are yours,
now and for ever. Amen.

2   Here where two, three or more are joined in breaking bread, Jesus is made known as the Other – as the prisoner, the wounded one, the sick, the thirsty, the naked, the homeless – who asks for our help. So I appeal to you, brothers and sisters, to offer yourselves, your lives and your labours, in solidarity with his reconciling love. Do not be conformed to

this age, but be transformed by the renewal of your will.

Sharing the meal

3   *Someone brings food, or just bread, to the table and says:*

Jesus Christ, the life of the world.

4   *Someone else places drink, or just water, on the table and says:*

Jesus Christ, the living water.

The meal is shared and eaten and people have a chance to exchange news and get to know newcomers.

Sharing concerns

Now follows an opportunity for people to mention things going on in the world, in their city, their neighbourhood, group or family, or personal concerns. Some may prefer to formulate a prayer or use a familiar petition such as the following:

Lord in your mercy

℞   **Hear our prayer.**

When all who wish have contributed, these words are said:

5   We become one, as we share our stories.

℞   **We celebrate that we are together.**

Joint activity

After the meal has been tidied away and any other practicalities are disposed of, the discussion, activity or project which has been planned is introduced with a reading or other appropriate material.

Reflection

6   Let us celebrate Christ, and examine ourselves in his presence. Christ was always ready to listen, always ready to talk.

℟   **Teach us to be ready to listen and to respond.**

7   Christ was at home everywhere, with everyone.

℟   **Help us to be open to all.**

8   Christ was not misled by stereotypes.

℟   **Help us to meet the reality behind the idea, the person behind the mask.**

9   Christ gave himself for others.

℟   **Help us to live for others.**

10   Christ preached what he lived.

℟   **May our deeds speak.**

11   Christ bore no grudges and forgives us all.

℟   **Forgive us, and teach us to forgive.**

12   Christ suffered and died for the world.

℞   **Give us courage to commit ourselves to life,
for all creation.**

Commitment

13   Shall we stand ...
Let us commit ourselves, as far as we can, to live by
the things we have seen and known in the power of
Jesus.

ALL   **We commit ourselves
to hold to the truth as it is in Jesus,
to support each other in good and ill.
to challenge evil with the power of love,
to offer the kingdom in political and economic
witness,
to work for the new community of all humanity,
and to risk ourselves in a lifestyle of sharing.**

14   The grace of the Lord Jesus be always with us.

ALL   **Amen.**

An agape celebrating the unity of mankind and re-committing the community to service.

Penitential and Bidding Prayers

1   For not being able to travel light
and being bogged down by material considerations

℞   **Forgive us, loving Creator.**

2   For the times when we have preferred the known
to facing the challenge of renewal

℞   **Forgive us, loving Creator.**

3   For being so fearful of change
and failing to grasp the need for continual transfor-
mation

℞   **Forgive us
and liberate us from fear and anxiety
so that we may do your will.**

4   Dom Helder Camara once prayed
that he might not make God a pillow
and prayer an eiderdown.
Help us to take heart
and have confidence in your guidance.
Lord hear us.

℞   **Lord, graciously hear us.**

5   Help us to leave behind all that hinders us
     in loving ourselves and our neighbour.
     Lord hear us.

℟   **Lord, graciously hear us.**

People can add their own prayers, then:

6   Let us say together:

ALL   **Forgive us, loving Creator, for our lack of courage.**
       Send forth your Spirit
       and make your new creation truly effective in us.
       Help all your people
       to work together in love and trust
       to build up the body of Christ.

Table Blessing

ALL   **Today we share bread and wine together,**
       as a sign that we are one humanity,
       as a pledge that we will work for justice,
       as a foretaste of that which can be,
       despite what is and what has been.

       May the holy Spirit that guides us all
       be present in this feast,
       taking this bread and wine,
       the concerns we have expressed,
       the lives that we lead
       and transforming them all
       for the unity of humankind
       and the service of love.

7   Blessed be the eternal Sustainer,
     working with soil and elements and human toil,
     bringing forth bread from the earth.

℞   **When the bodies of others are broken,
     we are broken.**

8   Blessed be the eternal Sustainer,
     working with soil and elements and human toil,
     making the fruit of the vine.

℞   **We are all kin,
     one blood.
     When the blood of others spills,
     our blood is spilled.**

*The wine and bread are passed round, and as they are
passed from one to the other, people may say, if they
wish:*

    The cup of compassion.

    The bread of sustenance.

23   A Congregational Agape

A form of grace before a celebration at which bread and wine are served as part of the meal.

1   *Someone says:*

Let us thank God for all creation.

ALL   **Lord, we thank you for the creation of the world.
We thank you for our life, the air we breathe,
the food we eat, the warmth we enjoy.**

2   *Someone else, or the leader, says:*

Let us thank God for our redemption.

ALL   **We confess our guilt and sin.
We thank you for the birth, life, death and resurrection of Jesus.
We thank you for the new life he has made available
to us.
We thank you for our new birth,
for our growth in grace,
and for the promise of eternal glory.**

3   *A third person, or the leader, says:*

Let us thank God for this celebration.

ALL   **Almighty God,
through your Son Jesus Christ we are redeemed.
We thank you for these gifts of bread and wine.
We thank you for his Body and Blood given for us.**

We pray that as we share these gifts,
so we may share his Body and Blood.

4   *Another person, or the leader, says:*

We praise and thank you Father

ALL   With the Holy Spirit through Jesus Christ our Lord,
Amen.

Symbols of Communion

A short grace before eating, based on the traditional Jewish blessing, which can be followed by the institution narrative *27 and become a Eucharist.

1   Let us drink from one cup
     to remember the joys and sorrows we share
     which are given us to grow together.

ALL   **Blessed are you, Lord,**
       God of all creation,
       who creates the fruit of the vine.

2   Let us eat this bread to remember our daily bread
     and our daily life together.
     May God hallow the small and ordinary things of
     life
     through his blessing.

ALL   **Blessed are you, Lord,**
       God of all creation,
       who brings forth bread from the earth.

Didsbury Rectory Agape

A liturgy thanking God for his gifts, especially the new covenant of his body and blood. It is suitable for a Christian group about to eat together.

1   *Someone says:*

We give you praise and thanks, Father,
for all you have done for the world ... (especially ...)

But even more we praise you for our Lord Jesus Christ,
as now we remember his life and ministry among us,
for all he has done for us and made possible in us.

℟   **We praise and thank you Lord.**

2   *Someone else, or the leader, says:*

Because you have brought us together to recall his saving work for us

℟   **We praise and thank you Lord.**

3   *Someone else says:*

Because he was born of Mary and sanctified our humanity, for this:

℟   **We praise and thank you Lord.**

4   *Anyone now recalls things for which we can thank God, using the following pattern:*

Because ... for this:

℟   **We praise and thank you Lord.**

5   *When these come to an end, someone else, or the leader, says:*

We praise you for the new covenant sealed by his blood,
for the forgiveness of our sins and the gift of a new life.

ALL   We therefore take this bread and this cup,
and we thank you, that in your fatherly mercy,
by our Saviour's promise
and with the help of your Holy Spirit,
it is the means by which we remember his holy sacrifice
and share in his body and blood.
So in faithful trust,
we offer ourselves a living sacrifice,
for worship and for service.
May your kingdom come, and your will be done,
in and through us all. Amen.

A prayerful liturgy involving readings on Jewish sacrifice and the priesthood of Jesus Christ, ending with a Eucharist.

Sacrifice

1   Reading from Leviticus [8:5–10, 12–13; 9:7–10, 22–4] on the ordination and sacrifice of Aaron.

2   *Someone takes some bread and holding it up says:*

Blessed are you, Lord, God of all creation. You nourish the whole world with goodness, tender love and mercy. Through your goodness we have this bread to offer, which earth has given and human hands have made. It will become for us the bread of life.

℞   **Blessed be God for ever!**

3   *Someone else takes some wine and holding it up over the food says:*

Blessed are you, Lord, God of all creation. You have made us a royal priesthood, a consecrated people. Through your goodness we have this wine to offer, the fruit of the vine and the work of human hands. It will become our spiritual drink.

℞   **Blessed be God for ever!**

Discussion may follow.

Failure

4   Reading from Ezekiel [34:1–12] where Yahweh condemns the shepherds of Israel.

Discussion may follow with extempore acts of penance, on the pattern:

5   We have failed to … (or something similar, always ending:)
… Lord have mercy.

℞   **Lord have mercy.**

Christian Priesthood

6   Reading from Hebrews [10:1–25] on the priesthood of Jesus Christ.

Celebration

7   The Lord be with you.

℞   **And also with you.**

8   Let us lift up our hearts.

℞   **We lift them up to the Lord.**

9   Let us give thanks to the Lord our God.

℞   **It is right and fitting.**

10   Father, all-powerful ever-living God, we should
      always and everywhere give you thanks. You
      anointed Jesus Christ, your only son as the eternal
      priest. He gave his life, death and resurrection in
      redemption for the human race by his one perfect
      sacrifice. As we eat and drink together, let us
      remember:

ALL   **On the same night that he was betrayed,
      the Lord Jesus took some bread,
      and thanked God for it,
      and broke it, and he said:
      'This is my body, broken for you.
      Do this as a memorial of me.'**

   The bread is broken and passed round.

11   Let us remember now, how after supper Jesus took
      the cup and said:

ALL   **'This cup is the new covenant in my blood.
      Whenever you drink it,
      do this as a memorial of me.'
      Until the Lord comes therefore
      every time we eat this bread and drink this cup
      we are proclaiming his death.**

   The cup is passed round.

   The celebration can end with the Our Father *or some
   other suitable prayer.*

*Institution Narrative

The story of the Last Supper arranged for group recitation. A short Eucharist, which may be preceded by readings and prayers.

1   When the hour came, he took his place at table, and
    the apostles with him.
    And he said to them:

℞   'I have longed to eat this Passover with you before I
    suffer,
    because, I tell you, I shall not eat again
    until it is fulfilled in the kingdom of God.'

2   *Pouring some wine:*

    Then, taking a cup, he gave thanks and said:

℞   'Take this, and share it among you,
    because from now on, I tell you, I shall not drink
    wine
    until the kingdom of God comes.'

3   *Taking some bread and breaking it:*

    Then he took some bread, and when he had given
    thanks he broke it and gave it to them, saying:

℞   'This is my body,
    which will be given for you.
    Do this as a memorial of me.'

4   *Taking the wine which has been poured out:*

He did the same with the cup after supper, and said:

℟   **'This is the covenant in my blood
which will be poured out for you.'**

5   Let us proclaim the mystery of faith!

℟   **When we eat this bread and drink this cup,
we proclaim your death Lord Jesus
until you come in glory.**

The sharing of the blessed bread and wine follows.

An attempt to reconstruct the Last Supper, with the traditional Jewish prayers used by Jesus together with his additions. Readings or discussion may come first. Note that two cups of wine are passed round, the second being the Cup of Blessing.

1   When the hour came, he took his place at table, and the apostles with him. And he said to them:

ALL   'I have longed to eat this Passover with you
       before I suffer,
       because, I tell you,
       I shall not eat again until the heavenly banquet,
       when all is fulfilled.'

2   *Pouring some wine:*

       Then, taking a cup, he gave thanks and said:

ALL   'Blessed are you Lord God of all creation.
       You create the fruit of the vine.
       Take this, and share it among you,
       because from now on, I tell you,
       I shall not drink wine until the kingdom of God
       comes.'

The wine is passed round.

3   *Someone else takes some bread and says:*

Then he took some bread, and gave thanks, saying:

ALL   'Blessed are you Lord God of all creation.
You bring forth bread from the earth.'

4   *Breaking the bread and passing it round:*

Then he broke the bread and gave it to them, saying:

ALL   'This is my flesh, which will be given for you.
Do this as a memorial of me.'

The bread is passed round and eaten.

5   *Then someone else takes the cup of wine, which has been replenished if necessary, and says:*

He did the same with the cup after supper, and said:

ALL   'Blessed are you Lord God of all creation.
You nourish us and the whole world
with goodness, grace and mercy.
We thank you for giving us
a good and ample land for our inheritance.
Have mercy on us your chosen people
and on Jerusalem, the place of your glory.
Blessed are you, Lord God, for you rebuild Jerusalem.'

6   Jesus then added these words:

ALL   'This is the covenant in my blood
which will be poured out for you.'

7   Let us proclaim the mystery of faith!

**ALL   When we eat this bread and drink this cup,
we proclaim your death Lord Jesus
until you come in glory.**

The sharing of the blessed wine follows.

29

*The Little Gidding Rite

The Eucharist of a modern ecumenical Christian community.

1   *The leader, or someone, says:*

Jesus prayed to the Father for his disciples, saying, 'May they be one, as you and I are one, that the world may know that you sent me.'

ALL   **Almighty God,**
through the sacrifice of your Son Jesus Christ,
you have revealed for us the way of eternal life.
Sanctify us in your truth,
and set us free to serve you in humble praise.

2   *Someone else, or the leader, says:*

On the night he was betrayed, Jesus took bread, gave thanks to God, broke it and said:

ALL   **'Take and eat. This is my body which is given for you.**
Do this in remembrance of me.'

3   *A third person, or the leader, says:*

In the same way he took the cup and said:

ALL   **'Drink this all of you.**
This is my blood of the new covenant,
which is shed for you and for many
for the forgiveness of sins.

Do this, as often as you drink it, in remembrance of
me.'
Father, in obedience to your Son Jesus Christ,
we celebrate with this bread and this cup
his victory on the cross,
lifting our hearts to you in joyful thanksgiving.
We praise you for your whole creation,
that through it we may see your glory;
and we thank you that in Jesus Christ
we die to sin and are raised to new life.

4   God calls us to be a kingdom of priests,
that the world may know his wonderful power.

ALL   May God fill us with the spirit of love,
faith and hope,
that we may grow in the image of Christ.

5   We break this bread to share in the body of Christ.

ALL   Though we are many
we are one body
because we share in one bread.

The bread and wine are shared.

An Advent Table Liturgy

30

An agape for use in Advent, using the traditional O antiphons from the old Roman vespers just before Christmas.

After suitable readings, each takes it in turn to recite one of the petitions:

1   Wisdom of the Most High,
ordering all things with strength and gentleness.

℞   **Come and teach us the way of truth!**

2   Ruler of the House of Israel,
who gave the Law to Moses on Sinai.

℞   **Come, and save us with outstretched arm!**

3   Root of Jesse, set up as a sign to the nations.

℞   **Come to save us and delay no more!**

4   Key of David, who opens the gates of the eternal kingdom.

℞   **Come to liberate from prison the captive who lives in darkness!**

5   Morning Star, radiance of eternal light, sun of justice.

℞   **Come and enlighten those who live in darkness and in the shadow of death!**

6   King of the nations and corner-stone of the Church.

℞   **Come and save us whom you made from the dust of the earth.**

7   Emmanuel, our king and law-giver.

℞   **Come and save us, Lord our God!**

The food is blessed as follows, each taking it in turn to recite one of the petitions:

1   Lord you have given us these gifts of food
        which we share in fellowship.

℞   **Come, Lord Jesus!**

2   Lord you said 'When two or three are gathered together,
        I am in your midst.'

℞   **Come, Lord Jesus!**

3   Lord you gave us an example
        and asked us to serve one another in love.

℞   **Come, Lord Jesus!**

4   Lord you said 'I am the bread which came down from heaven.'

℞   **Come, Lord Jesus!**

5   After your resurrection from the dead
        you revealed yourself to your disciples in the breaking of bread.

℞   **Come, Lord Jesus!**

6   Let us proclaim the mystery of faith:

℞   **When we eat this bread and drink this cup
we proclaim your death Lord Jesus
until you come in glory!**

*The bread is passed round for each to break a piece off
and wine is shared.*

31   An Easter Table Liturgy

An agape in celebration of the risen Christ!

First Reading: The Road to Emmaus (Luke 24:13ff.).
After the reading:

> Reader: Christ is risen!
>
> ℟   **Christ is risen indeed, alleluya!**

Second Reading: Breakfast by the Lake (John 21:1–14).
After the reading:

> Reader: Christ is risen!
>
> ℟   **Christ is risen indeed, alleluya!**

The food is blessed as follows, each taking it in turn to recite one of the petitions:

1   Lord you have given us these gifts of food
     which we share in fellowship.

℟   **Show yourself to us Lord.**

2   Lord you said 'When two or three are gathered together,
     I am in your midst.'

℟   **Show yourself to us Lord.**

3   Lord you gave us an example and asked us to serve
     one another in love.

℟   **Show yourself to us Lord.**

4   Lord you said 'I am the bread which came down
     from heaven.'

℟   **Show yourself to us Lord.**

5   After your resurrection from the dead
     you revealed yourself to your disciples in the
     breaking of bread.

℟   **Show yourself to us Lord.**

6   Let us proclaim the mystery of faith:

℟   **When we eat this bread and drink this cup
     we proclaim your death Lord Jesus
     until you come in glory!**

*The bread is passed around for each to break a piece off
and wine is poured into each glass.*

*From Corinthians

A form of grace before and after meals based on St Paul's account of the institution of the Eucharist.

Before the meal

1 As we eat and drink together,
  let us remember:

ALL **On the same night that he was betrayed,
  the Lord Jesus took some bread,
  and thanked God for it,
  and broke it, and he said:
  'This is my body, broken for you.
  Do this as a memorial of me.'**

The bread is broken and passed round.

Towards the end of the meal

2 Let us remember now, how after supper
  Jesus took the cup and said:

ALL **'This cup is the new covenant in my blood.
  Whenever you drink it,
  do this as a memorial of me.'
  Until the Lord comes, therefore,
  every time we eat this bread and drink this cup
  we are proclaiming his death.**

The cup is passed round.

Emmaus Liturgy

A short liturgy involving the sharing of broken bread as a symbol of humankind's unity in Jesus.

1   A Reading from Luke 24:28–32:

Arriving at the village of Emmaus, Jesus seemed to be continuing on. The couple insisted he at least stay and have some food with them, so he did. It was while they were together at table that Jesus took bread and spoke the blessing.

The bread is held up and all stretch their hands towards it.

ALL   Thank you God for this life-giving bread
to strengthen and sustain us.

There is but one bread
but many of us here.

Because we all have a share of this one bread,
we form a single body.

So break, take and eat.
This is in communion with the body of Christ.

The bread is broken and shared.

34   *An Anaphora for Today

A modern eucharistic prayer, perhaps preceded by readings, discussion and prayer.

1   This is the moment for giving thanks.

2   This is the moment for remembrance.

3   Let us remember why we are here.

ALL   We are here because we are Christians,
because we have been drawn together by the Spirit
whom Jesus said he would send into the world
to unite us all
and to lead us into the way of truth,
to be present among us
until the consummation of the world.

We then are the Church.
We are the body of Christ.

4   Let us remember at this time
all those who are united with us;

5   And let us give thanks for that bond of union
which we now celebrate.

6   Let us remember our past,
and give thanks for what we have become.

7   Let us give thanks for the whole universe
    and especially for our creation
    and the life that is in us.

8   Let us remember our future,
    and give thanks for all that is to happen to us.

9   Let us give thanks for the consummation of all
    things,
    which the Spirit is working out in us.

10 And now, in thanksgiving and remembrance,
    let us invoke the Spirit
    to bless this bread and wine,
    so that when we share it among ourselves
    we are sharing what we ourselves are and shall be,
    the body of Christ.

ALL **For we remember how Jesus, before he died,
    to bring us life by sharing our mortality,
    ate this meal with his friends,
    and in thanksgiving blessed the bread
    and shared it with them, saying,
    'Eat this.
    It is my body.'**

    **And afterwards he blessed the cup of wine,
    and shared it with them, saying,**

    **'Drink this.
    It is my blood.
    When you do this, remember me.'**

11 And so this meal becomes a sacrifice, a holy
    thing.

12   For by sharing this bread and wine
we remember him and what he was.

ALL   We remember ourselves and what we are.
We remember the glory of the whole universe
and what we shall all become;
and filled with joy and thankfulness
we give praise to God the Father,
and to his Son, Jesus Christ,
and to the Spirit of love and holiness
who has come to dwell in us
for ever and ever. Amen.

A Johannine Agape

35

From the Fourth Gospel's meditation on Jesus, the Bread of Life, with whom we are called to union.

1   The Word was made flesh and lived among us.

℟   **We saw his glory,
the glory that is his as the only Son of the Father,
full of grace and truth.**

2   As you sent him into the world,

℟   **So he sent us into the world.**

3   For our sake he offered himself,

℟   **So that we too might be consecrated in truth.
Consecrate us in the truth,
for your word is truth.**

4   Jesus said, 'I tell you most solemnly,
everybody who believes has eternal life.'

℟   **I am the bread of life.
Your fathers ate the manna in the desert
and they are dead,
But this is the bread that comes down from heaven,
so that we may eat it and not die.**

5   I am the living bread which has come down from
     heaven.

℟   **Anyone who eats this bread**
     will live for ever.

6   The bread that I shall give you is my flesh,
     for the life of the world.

7   I tell you most solemnly,
     if you do not eat the flesh of the son of man
     and drink his blood,
     you will not have life in you.

8   My flesh is real food and my blood is real drink.
     All who eat my flesh and drink my blood
     live in me
     and I live in them.

9   As I who am sent by the living Father
     draw life from the Father,
     so whoever eats me
     will draw life from me.

10   This is the bread come down from heaven.

℟   **Anyone who eats this bread**
     will live for ever.

11   May we all be one, Father.

℟   **May we all be one in you,**
     as you are in Christ
     and he is in you,
     so that the world may believe that you sent him.

12   He gave us the glory that you gave him.

℟   **So that we may be one
as you and Christ are one
with Christ in us and you in Christ.
May we be completely one,
that the world will realize you sent him,
and that he loves them
even as you love him.**

13   He made your name known to us.

℟   **May we continue to make it known,
that we may show your love for him,
and that he himself may live in us. Amen.**

36

*Celebrating the Kingdom

A modern eucharistic prayer, looking forward to the coming of the kingdom on earth, which we are called to build.

1   The love and peace of the Lord be with you.

℟   **And also with you.**

2   Let us lift up our hearts
     to give thanks and praise to the Lord.

℟   **It is right for us to do so.**

3   We give you thanks and praise
     that through you
     the vision of the kingdom has come to all humanity.
     That vision you proclaimed in the synagogue at
     Nazareth.

4   In fidelity to this vision
     we have left the security of the Age of Faith
     and gone forth into the desert of the modern world.

5   We have left the fleshpots of certainty
     to live in the wasteland of moral relativism.

6   It is in this desolation
     that we can build the new Jerusalem
     and make the desert bloom like the rose.

7   In this celebration we bring together
     the future and the past:
     the past which was your historical life,
     the future which can be our making of your presence
     in the world.

8   It is through this re-enactment
     that we foreshadow the messianic banquet –

9   when all humanity shall have its fill –
     when all will sit at the welcome table.

10   We proclaim that through you we have the power
     to create heaven on earth.

11   Swords can be beaten into ploughshares
     and nations not learn war any more.

12   We proclaim the salvation of humanity.
     Through you, it no longer has any need of illusion.

13   It can have faith in itself.
     It has come of age.
     It is able to accept sole responsibility for the world.

ALL The night before you died,
     you showed us how much you loved us.
     When you were at supper,
     you took bread,
     gave thanks and praise,
     broke it and gave it to your disciples, saying,

     'Take this all of you and eat it.
     This is my body which will be given up for you.'

     When supper was ended,
     you took the cup that was filled with wine,
     gave thanks and gave it to your friends and said,

'Take this all of you
and drink from it,
the blood of the new and everlasting covenant.
It will be shed for you and for all
so that evil can be overcome.'

14   We do this in memory of you.

ALL   **Christ has died.**
        Christ is risen.
        Christ will come again!

The bread and wine are shared.

15   Through this coming to us, Lord,
        and your presence in our bodies,
        we celebrate your death until you come.

16   You died that the kingdom might live.

17   Only through this death
        could you unite yourself with us in love.

18   Only through this *kenosis* could your transcendence
        become a possibility for humanity.

19   Only if God became human
        could the human become divine.

20   In you we see that God is wholly human.

21   Let us now give the sign of peace
        as a foreshadowing of peace on earth.

The peace is exchanged.

22   Dear Lord, we have renewed our union with you.

23   We have made more real your presence in our lives.

24   You have given yourself to us unreservedly.

25   You have thrown in your lot with us.

26   We know that with you as our brother
there is nothing good we cannot do.

27   We have through this celebration
re-established love
as the measure of all things in our lives.

28   Let us go forth refreshed and reanimated
from this repast:

29   to show all humanity the love and truth
you have in everyone;

30   to bring them the good news.

ALL   **Let us go forth and build the kingdom. Amen.**

37 *A Eucharistic Prayer

A modern eucharistic prayer, to follow readings and discussion.

1   Let us pray together:

ALL   **The love and peace of the Lord be with us all.**

2   We believe in the power of the Spirit to bring us new life.

ALL   **Let us therefore lift up our hearts and minds
above our cares and fears.**

3   With love for his friends, on the night before he died:

ALL   **Christ took bread
and giving thanks,
broke it
and gave it to the disciples, saying,
'Take. Eat.
This is my body which is given for you.
Do this in remembrance of me.'**

       **After supper, Christ took the cup,
and again giving thanks,
gave it to the disciples, saying,
'Drink this cup all of you.
This is my blood of the new covenant
which is shed for you and many
for the forgiveness of sin.
Do this as often as you drink it
in remembrance of me.'**

Glory to you Christ.
Your death we show forth.
Your resurrection we proclaim.
Your coming we celebrate. Amen.

4   We pray with confidence in the words our Saviour taught us:

ALL   **Our Father …**

5   We who are many are one body in Christ.

ALL   **For we all share in the brokenness of life**
and we all share in the bread of life
and the wine of the healing cup.

The sharing of bread and wine follows.

6   Let us go forth, refreshed and animated by this Eucharist, to share with humanity, the love and trust you have in everyone – to share the good news.

ALL   **Let us go forth to build the kingdom on earth**
here and now. Amen.

38   *Praying for the World

A modern eucharistic prayer, asking for reconciliation and unity, for renewal and peace.

1   The love and peace of God be with you.

℟   **And also with you.**

2   Let us lift up our hearts to give thanks and praise to God.

ALL   **It is right for us to do so.**
All-powerful and ever-living God,
we do well
always and everywhere to give you thanks
through Jesus Christ our Lord.
Through Christ you bring us to the knowledge of your truth,
that we may be united by one faith and one baptism to become his body.

3   From first to last it has been your work
to reconcile us men and women to yourself through Christ,
and to enlist us in the service of reconciliation.
God was in Christ
reconciling the world to himself,
no longer holding our misdeeds against us.

4   Remembering Christ,
who died on the cross,
believing in him who has risen from the dead,
and recognizing him here in our brothers and sisters,
we obey his command.

ALL   **We offer this bread and wine.**
We offer ourselves
to be used in the work of peace.

5   Send down your Spirit of life and power,
glory and love,
upon this people
and upon this bread and wine.

6   So that the bread which we break
may be our communion in the body of Christ,
and the cup that we bless and share
may be our communion in the blood of Christ,
that the risen Lord may live in us
and we may live in him.

7   On the night he was betrayed,
he took bread,
broke it,
and gave it to his disciples saying,

ALL   **'Take this all of you and eat it.**
This is my body
which will be given up for you.'

8   In the same way he took the cup saying,

ALL 'Take this all of you and drink from it.
This is the cup of my blood,
the blood of the new and everlasting covenant.
It will be shed for you and for all
so that sins may be forgiven.
Do this in memory of me.'

9   God of love,
as we share this one bread and one cup,
we pray that all the barriers and walls which divide us
may be broken down;

10 that here a daughter shall be reconciled to her
mother,
and a father to his son,

11 that swords may be beaten into ploughshares
and wars abolished from the earth,
that all those who take up the sword may be
disarmed,

12 that we may be liberated from discrimination
and form the human race of Jesus Christ,

13 that we may plant the garden of peace on this planet
and renew the old wastes,
that we shall rebuild our broken world together
under the roof of Christ, our peace;

ALL through him, with him, in him,
in the unity of the Holy Spirit,
all glory and honour is yours,
almighty God, for ever and ever. Amen.

All share in broken bread and wine.

A modern eucharistic prayer, giving thanks for all God's blessings.

1   The love and peace of God be with you.

℟   **And also with you.**

2   Let us lift up our hearts to give thanks and praise to God.

℟   **It is right for us to do so.**

3   We give you praise and thanks,
     God Creator of us all,
     that you have given us space and time
     to live, love and worship you.

4   Blessed are you in all the things you have made,
     in plants and in animals,
     and above all, in us your people,
     the wonder of your creation.

5   Blessed are you for the food we eat,
     the air we breathe,
     the home we live in,
     and the friends we have.

6   Blessed are you
     that you have given us eyes to see your goodness
     in the things you have made,
     and ears to hear your Word,
     hands that we may touch and bless and understand.

7   But most of all we bless you
     for your Son, Jesus Christ,
     your Word of love, truth and life.

8   Therefore we praise you with all the living.
     We bow down before you and adore you saying:

ALL   **Holy, holy holy,**
           God of all creation.
           Blessed is the One who is in our midst.
           We bless your name.

9   We now ask you, eternal God, to send your Spirit of
     love, joy and peace, to change these gifts of bread
     and wine into the body and blood of Jesus Christ,
     your Son.

10   The night before he died, Jesus showed us how much
     he loved us. When he was at supper with his disci-
     ples, he took bread and gave you thanks and praise.
     Then he broke the bread, gave it to his friends and
     said:

ALL   **Take this, all of you, and eat it.**
           This is my body, which will be given up for you.

11   When supper was ended, Jesus took the cup that
     was filled with wine. He thanked you, gave it to his
     friends and said:

ALL   **Take this, all of you, and drink from it.**
           This is the cup of my blood,
           the blood of the new and everlasting covenant.
           It will be shed for you and for all
           so that sins may be forgiven.
           Do this in memory of me.

12   Eternal God, listen to our prayers. Send your Spirit
      to all of us who share in this eucharistic celebration.
      May your Spirit bring us closer together and show
      us the true meaning of love. Keep us in communion
      of mind and heart with all your servants who hold
      and teach our faith. Grant to us, your people, the
      courage to live our lives in the image of your Son.

13   Increase in us a concern for those whom you love,
      for the lonely, for the poor, for the homeless, for
      those we discriminate against, and for all who are in
      need, that we may labour in your name to restore
      them their rightful dignity as your daughters and
      sons.

14   We pray that before the eyes of all, we may live your
      gospel and be the sign of Christ's presence, that thus
      we may truly be the body of Jesus Christ, serving
      one another out of love for you.

ALL   **So, eternal God,**
      may you always be pleased with us,
      even as you were pleased
      to look upon the face of your Son, Jesus Christ.

      For through him,
      and with him,
      and in him,
      you are blessed and praised,
      in the unity of the Holy Spirit,
      today and all days until eternity. Amen.

All share in the bread and wine.

15   Let us end our celebration by saying:

ALL   Remain with us, O God,
and grant us your peace.
There is no strength but in you.
There is no unity but in your house.
Under your hand we shall pass all danger.
You are our mother and our father.
You are our home. Amen.

May the blessing of the Holy Trinity rest upon us,
and may all our work and worship be done in God's name.

And may the grace of our Lord Jesus Christ,
and the love of God,
and the fellowship of the Holy Spirit
be with us all evermore. Amen.

* A Eucharistic Thanksgiving

A modern eucharistic prayer focussing on the person of Jesus.

After a suitable preparation, readings, etc.:

1   Lord our God,
    gathered together here around you,
    we remember the old story
    which has been told down the ages
    of Jesus of Nazareth,
    a man who dared to call you Abba, Father,
    and taught us to do the same thing.

2   O God,
    we thank you for this man
    who has changed the face of the earth,
    because he spoke of a great vision,
    of the kingdom of God which will come one day,
    a kingdom of freedom, love and peace,
    your kingdom,
    the perfection of your creation.

3   We remember that wherever Jesus came,
    women and men rediscovered their humanity,
    and so we were filled with new riches,
    so that we could give one another
    new courage in our lives.

4   We remember how he spoke to people,
about a lost coin,
about a sheep that had strayed,
about a lost son,
of all those who are lost and no longer count,
who are out of sight and out of mind,
the weak and the poor,
all those who are captive, unknown and unloved.

5   We recall that he went to search
for all who were lost,
for those who were saddened and out in the cold,
and how he always took their side
without forgetting others.

6   And that cost him his life,
because the mighty of the earth
would not tolerate it,
and yet,
he knew that he was understood
and accepted by you.
He saw himself confirmed by you in love.

7   So he became one with you,
and so freed from himself
he could live a life of liberation for others.

ALL   **And we remember how he,
who loved us so much
and was one with you his father,
on the last night of his life on earth
took bread in his hands,
blessed and broke
and shared it at table with his friends, saying,
'This is my body, given for you.'**

And what he did filled his heart.
He also took the cup at table,
gave thanks and praised you Father, and said,
'Drink this cup all of you with me,
for this is my loving covenant with you,
my blood which is shed for your reconciliation,
the cup of liberation and happiness.'

So when we eat this bread together
and drink of this cup,
we do it in remembrance of him, your Son,
who is servant and liberator of us all,
now and ever and beyond death.

8   Therefore we also think of the many who have gone
    from us,
    all the people whom we have loved so much …

    You are their life now and always.

9   We think too of the world,
    of all who love us in life.
    Even the powerful, who have in their hands
    the destiny of men and women,
    often without knowing them,
    the rulers of the world and of the Church.

10 Help them and us,
    so that we may make this earth
    a better home for us all,
    so that we may make peace and be one,
    as you, Father, are in your Son,
    and he is in you.

11 So send your Spirit upon us
    and upon these gifts,
    the good Spirit from you and your Son,
    that it may inspire us when we continue to follow Jesus,
    Jesus from whom we have learnt to be free,
    free from powers which estrange us,
    free to do good.

12 As best we could, we have done what Jesus, your witness,
    who knows our hearts, commands us to do,
    to celebrate his memory.

ALL In praise and thanks to you,
     almighty God,
     in the unity of the Holy Spirit,
     now too we may and dare,
     through him and with him and in him,
     to pray together as he taught us:

     Our Father …

     Strengthened and encouraged
     we now dare to pass round this bread and cup,
     the sacrament of faith.

The bread and wine are shared.

13 We pray you our God,

ALL Make what we have done in memory of Jesus,
     who was filled by your Spirit,
     a living and effective sign
     of salvation and wholeness,
     a sign of mutual and honest love,
     a sign of freedom, peace and righteousness for all,
     a sign of love for you,
     O God our liberator.

A modern eucharistic prayer celebrating our incorporation into Jesus Christ.

1   Eternal Wisdom, source of our being,
and goal of all our longing,
we praise and give you thanks
because you have created us, men and women,
together in your image,
to cherish your world and seek your face.

2   Divided and disfigured by sin,
while we were yet helpless,
you emptied yourself of power,
and took upon you our unprotected flesh.
You laboured with us upon the cross
and have brought us forth
to the hope of resurrection.

ALL   Holy, holy, holy,
vulnerable God,
heaven and earth are full of your glory,
hosanna in the highest.
Blessed is the one who comes in the name of God.
Hosanna in the highest.

Blessed is our brother Jesus,
who before his suffering
earnestly desired to eat with his companions
the Passover of liberation;
who on the night that he was betrayed
took bread, gave thanks,

broke it and said,
'This is my body, which is for you.
Do this to remember me.'

In the same way also
he took the cup after supper and said,
'This cup is the new covenant in my blood.
Do this, whenever you drink it,
to remember me.'

Christ has died.
Christ is risen.
Christ will come again.

3 Therefore, as we eat this bread and drink this cup,
we are proclaiming Christ's death until he comes.
In the body broken and the blood poured out,
we restore to memory and hope
the broken and unremembered victims
of tyranny and sin;
and we long for the bread of tomorrow
and the wine of the age to come.

4 Come then, life-giving Spirit of our God,
brood over these bodily things,
and make us one body with Christ,
that we may labour with creation
to be delivered from its bondage to decay
into the glorious liberty
of all the children of God.

Table Blessings

After sharing the bread and wine:

5   Eternal God

ALL   Our beginning and our end,
be our starting point and our heaven
and accompany us in this day's journey.
Use our hands
to do the work of your creation,
and use our lives
to bring others the new life
which you give this world in Jesus Christ,
Redeemer of all. Amen.

42

*A Christian Kiddush

A Christian form for a Friday night celebration at supper, recalling the ancient Jewish custom still in use. The atmosphere should be easy and relaxed.

Lighting the candles

1   Let us pray:

ALL   Blessed are you, Lord God of all creation,
you have made us holy by your commandments.
Blessed is the Lord who is to be blessed
for ever and ever.

The candles are now lit. While this is happening the following is said by all.

ALL   God is my light and my salvation;
whom shall I fear?
God is the strength of my life;
of whom shall I be afraid?

Loving God, you are the light of the world.
In your mercy you give light to the earth
and all who live in it.
May the brightness of this light illumine our hearts
with the spirit of faith and love.
Let the light of your presence guide us,
for in your light do we see light.
Bless with your spirit people everywhere
so that happiness and peace may ever be with them.
Amen.

Prayer for help

ALL   Have mercy on us, eternal God, in your goodness.
Grant us pardon and forgiveness of all our sins,
time to change our life,
and the help and comfort of your spirit.
Renew our joy and grant us your blessing.

Prayer for fellowship

ALL   God, your infinite power and wisdom are reflected
in the variety of creation.
We see your work also
in the differences that are found
in the minds of your people.
We pray to you for our brothers and sisters.
Take them all under the sheltering wings of your love.
Let us see, we pray,
that our many differences of thought and belief
are implanted by you,
and let us strive more zealously
to be one in love and tolerance,
one in the desire to know and do your will.

Readings

These are usually but not always taken from Scripture. After the readings, some time is left for silent reflection. After a short while, people may want to share with others what the readings meant to them. It is important to keep a feeling of worship during that period. Experience has shown that it is sometimes better to leave any discussion of issues until afterwards. Bidding Prayers and Sign of Peace may follow, using familiar forms.

Prayer over bread and wine

Bread and wine are placed on the table.

ALL   Blessed are you, Lord God of all creation,
you have made us holy by your love
and accepted us as your daughters and sons.
In your love you have gathered us, your people,
to praise the work of creation,
and to celebrate our freedom and salvation
which Jesus gained for us.

Let us remember the exodus from Egypt,
our release from the slavery of sin.

You have chosen us and made us holy.
You have given us these gifts
so that we may praise you and thank you,
this day and every day. Amen.

Reading from St Paul's Letter to the Corinthians

2   As we prepare to eat this bread and drink this wine,
let us recall the words of St Paul in his letter to the
Christians at Corinth [1 Cor. 11:23–6 (JB)]:

For this is what I received from the Lord, and in turn
passed on to you: that on the same night that he was
betrayed, the Lord Jesus took some bread, and
thanked God for it and broke it, and he said, 'This is
my body, which is for you; do this as a memorial of
me'. In the same way he took the cup after supper,
and said, 'This cup is the new covenant in my blood.
Whenever you drink it, do this as a memorial of
me.' Until the Lord comes, therefore, every time you
eat this bread and drink this cup, you are
proclaiming his death.

Table Blessings

Sharing of bread and wine

ALL   Blessed are you, Lord God of all creation,
through your goodness you have given us our daily
bread.
You are the bread of life.

All share the broken bread.

ALL   Blessed are you, Lord God of all creation,
maker of the fruit of the vine.
You are the cup of life.

All share the cup.

A period of silence may follow before the final prayer:

Final thanksgiving

ALL   God of love,
we thank you for the gifts on our table,
for the fellowship of our friends,
for the forgiveness you grant us
and for the unending love you show us.

Our Father ...

The grace of our Lord Jesus Christ
and the love of God,
and the fellowship of the Holy Spirit
be with us all evermore.

Let us go to work for peace and love in God's world.
Amen.

43

*A Shorter Christian Seder

An elaborated form of Christian Passover meal to be celebrated within a supper, with elements from the Jewish Passover and the last supper of Jesus and his disciples.

Before eating

When all are seated and the meal is prepared, after a Haggadah (optional), Psalm 113 (Grail version) is said by two groups:

A   Praise, O servants of the Lord;
       praise the name of the Lord.

B   May the name of the Lord be blessed,
       both now and for evermore.

A   From the rising of the sun to its setting
       praised be the name of the Lord!

B   High above all the nations is the Lord,
       high above the heavens his glory.

A   Who is like the Lord, our God,
       who has risen on high to his throne

B   yet stoops from the heights to look down,
       to look down upon heaven and earth?

A   From the dust he lifts up the lowly;
       from the dungheap he raises the poor

B   to set them in the company of rulers
       yes, with the rulers of his people.

A   To the childless wife he gives a home
       and gladdens her heart with children.

B   **Glory be to the Father and to the Son**
        and to the Holy Spirit

A   **As it was in the beginning is now and ever shall be**
        World without end. Amen.

The blessing is said by the president:

1   Blessed are you, Lord, God of all creation;
      you bring forth bread from the earth.

*The president, or someone else, breaks the bread, keeps a
piece and passes the rest round for people to eat at once,
saying:*

2   Jesus, at the last supper with his friends,
      added these words:
      'Take; this is my flesh.
      Do this in remembrance of me.'

After eating

*When the meal is over, the Cup of Blessing, prepared at
the beginning of the meal with some water and left
prominently during the meal, is brought forward and
blessed with the traditional words by one of those present
as follows:*

3   Let us give thanks to the Lord our God.

℞   **Blessed be the name of the Lord**
      from this time forth for evermore.

4   Let us bless God whose generosity has given us food.

℞   **Blessed be God for ever!**

5 Blessed are you, Lord, God of all creation;
you nourish the entire world
with goodness, tender love and mercy.

℞ **Blessed be God for ever!**

6 We give you thanks, Lord our God,
for you have given us a desirable land for our
inheritance;
you brought us out of Egypt and freed us from
slavery.
You gave your people a covenant;
you taught us your law,
and you fill us with life and food.

℞ **Blessed be God for ever!**

7 Lord our God, Jesus and his disciples
prayed that you should have mercy
on your people Israel,
on your holy city Jerusalem,
on Zion, the dwelling place of your glory.

℞ **Blessed be God for ever!**

8 Jesus then took the cup and blessed it saying:
'This is my blood, of the new covenant,
shed for you.
Do this in remembrance of me.'

The cup is passed around for all to drink.

9 Let us proclaim the mystery of faith.

℞ **When we eat this bread and drink this cup,
we proclaim your death Lord Jesus
until you come in glory.**

Psalm 115 (Grail version) follows:

A   I trusted, even when I said
       'I am sorely afflicted,'

B   and when I said in my alarm:
       'There is no one I can trust.'

A   How can I repay the Lord
       for his goodness to me?

B   The cup of salvation I will raise;
       I will call on the Lord's name.

A   My vows to the Lord I will fulfil
       before all his people.

B   O precious in the eyes of the Lord
       is the death of his faithful.

A   Your servant, Lord, your servant am I;
       you have loosened my bonds.

B   A thanksgiving sacrifice I make;
       I will call on the Lord's name.

A   My vows to the Lord I will fulfil
       before all his people

B   in the courts of the house of the Lord,
       in your midst, O Jerusalem.

A   Glory be to the Father and to the Son
       and to the Holy Spirit

B   as it was in the beginning is now and ever shall be
       world without end. Amen.

44   *A Simple Communion

A modern ecumenical eucharistic prayer.

1   We are here because we share a common faith.
    God the Father created us.
    God the Son, Jesus Christ, makes us whole;
    God the Holy Spirit strengthens us.

ALL   **Our Father ...**

Readings may now follow.

2   Let us confess our sins to God and before each other.

ALL   **Almighty God, we are often foolish and not honest
      with you, with each other, or with ourselves.
      We confess to you in the presence of this company
      that we have been selfish
      and sometimes we have hurt each other.
      We are sorry. We seek forgiveness.
      We seek new life.**

After a time of silence:

3   We say together:

ALL   **God forgives us,
      lifts the burdens from our shoulders,
      and gives us time for change of life.**

4   Friends, let us also forgive each other
    and love one another, for love is of God.

ALL   **May the peace of God be with us.**

Table Blessings

The peace may be exchanged and intercessions may follow. Bread and wine are then placed on the table, if not already there.

5   We offer this bread and this wine.

ALL   **Lord, accept these offerings
as tokens of all the good things you give us.
We give thanks to you for your whole creation.
We give thanks for Jesus, born into a human family.
He shared our suffering
and was cruelly killed by his fellow men.**

6   He told us to remember his death
and his rising from the dead, which gives us life.

ALL   **We remember his death and rising from the dead.
Our lives are changed by the knowledge
that he is alive and with us.**

7   On the night Jesus was betrayed,
he had supper with his friends.
He took the loaf of bread,
gave thanks and broke it in pieces.
He shared it with them and said:

ALL   **'This is my body, given for you.
Do this in remembrance of me.'**

8   After supper he took the cup of wine
and shared it with them, saying:

ALL   **'Drink from it, all of you.
This is my blood of the covenant,
which is poured out for many
for the forgiveness of sins.'**

Take, Bless, Break, Share

9   As we share this bread and wine,
    may we also share in the life of Jesus
    and receive the Holy Spirit, giving freedom and
    power.

ALL   Come, risen Lord. Live in us that we may live in you.

10   *Breaking the bread into small pieces:*

    The gifts of God to share among us.

ALL   Though there are many of us,
      we are one body because we share the one bread.

*The bread and wine are passed round. After a time of
silence:*

11   We say together:

ALL   The grace of our Lord, Jesus Christ,
      the love of God,
      and the fellowship of the Holy Spirit,
      be with us all.

12   The Lord is with us. Let us go in peace.

ALL   We go in the name of Christ. Amen!

*A CRM Liturgy

45

A modern form of Eucharist.

1   Let us pray together:

ALL   **Peace be with us all.**

**For all our faults and failings,
for our failures in love towards other people,
for all those things which we have left undone,
have mercy upon us, eternal God,
in your goodness.**

**Help us to amend our lives,
to see the needs of other people,
to oppose the domination of some by others,
and to care for your world,
that your justice may fill the earth.**

2   We hold before you especially …

3   We thank you for …

4   In our Lord's own words, we say:

ALL   **Our Father …**

5   Christ is our peace.
He has reconciled us to God in one body by the cross.
We meet in his name and share his peace.

6   For he came to preach the good news to the poor,
to proclaim release to those who are held captive,
that the blind may receive their sight,
and the oppressed may be set at liberty.

All exchange the kiss of peace.

7   Blessed are you, God of the universe,
you have made us holy by your love
and accepted us as your daughters and sons.
In your love you have gathered us, your people,
to praise the work of creation
and to celebrate our freedom and salvation
which Jesus gained for us.

8   You have chosen us and made us holy.
You have given us these gifts
that we may praise you and thank you,
this day and every day.

ALL   **Amen.**

9   As we prepare to eat this bread and drink this wine, let us recall the word of St Paul in his letter to the Christians at Corinth. 'For this is what I received from the Lord and in turn passed on to you: that on the same night that he was betrayed, the Lord Jesus took some bread, thanked God for it, broke it and said 'This is my body which is for you. Do this as a memorial of me.'

10   In the same way he took the cup after supper and said, 'This cup is the new covenant in my blood. Whenever you drink it, do this as a memorial of me.' Until the Lord comes therefore, every time you eat this bread and drink this cup, you are proclaiming his death.'

Table Blessings

Someone breaks the bread and says:

11   We break this bread to share in the body of Christ.

ALL   **Though we are many, we are one body,
because we all share in the one bread.**

All share in the broken bread.

12   We share this cup to share in the life of Christ.

ALL   **Always, wherever we may be,
we carry with us in our body the death of Christ,
so that the life of Christ too
may always be seen in our body.**

All share the cup.

13   Blessed are you, God of the universe.

ALL   **We thank you for the gifts on our table,
for the fellowship of our friends,
for the forgiveness you grant us
and for the unending love you show us.**

**The grace of our Lord Jesus Christ,
and the love of God,
and the fellowship of the Holy Spirit
be with us all evermore. Amen.**

14   Let us go in the name of the Lord

ALL   **to work for peace and love in God's world. Amen.**

46

*A CRM Canon

A eucharistic prayer, celebrating our call to share in God's work by creating community. Readings and discussion should come first.

1 The Lord be with you.

℞ **And also with you.**

2 Let us lift up our hearts.

℞ **We have lifted them up to the Lord.**

3 Let us give thanks to the Lord our God.

℞ **It is right and just.**

4 We thank you, Lord God,
for your loving trust in your people.
In creation, you first clothed us with dignity,
called us, not things, but sons and daughters,
and saw that we were very good.

5 You did not hesitate, even then,
to offer what was most intimate to yourself,
a share in your creative power.

6 Thus from the beginning
it has ever been our vocation
to fashion this world and ourselves
in the image of your love.

7   Since today, as never before,
    your work is in our hands,
    we, the whole of creation,
    in all our frailty and mystery,
    with all our races and peoples
    join hands around your table,
    in doubt, in love,
    in risk, in hope.

8   We offer you thanks in a new way,
    not by being lifted out of what is human,
    but by daring to be what we truly are,
    the work of your loving hands,

9   God-touching and frail,
    but possessing a beauty beyond belief,
    we find the courage to stand and say:

ALL   **Holy, holy, holy Lord,**
          God of power and might.
          Heaven and earth are full of your glory.
          Hosanna in the highest.
          Blessed is he who comes in the name of the Lord.
          Hosanna in the highest.

10   Blessed are you, God,
     for your loving trust in men and women.
     When we lost faith in the dignity of our call,
     when we doubted your love and cursed your law,
     you sent not your wrath to crush us
     but your Son to be our brother.

11   He has come to our table and eaten our bread.
     He has walked in the cool of the evening
     with men and women he called his friends.

12   His tears were real, his joys intense;
his prayer: that we might learn to love one another.
Yet the sorrow which finally crushed him
was one in which we all played a part.

13   For on the night before he died
he was betrayed by one man,
by one who offered him a kiss,
by one who called him 'friend'.

ALL   **Yet on that very night,
he gave the greatest proof of his love.
He took bread in his hands
and lifted his eyes to you,
God his almighty Father.
He thanked you,
blessed and broke the bread,
and gave it to his friends with the words,
'This is my body which is broken for you.'
When the supper was ended, he took the cup,
gave thanks and shared it with them, saying,
'This is the cup of my blood,
the blood of the new covenant.
This blood shall be shed for you and for all
so that sins may be forgiven.**

14   Now, whenever we eat this bread and drink from this cup,
we recall the days when the Lord walked this earth.

15   We remember especially that night when he proved his love
in one final, total, offering
by laying down his life for his friends.

16   Living, he taught us how to live.
     Dying, he truly set us free.

ALL   Therefore, Lord our God, '
      we gather about this table
      in the name of of your Son,
      at his own request.
      We place here bread and wine,
      simple gifts,
      signs of our faith in your world.

      We are conscious
      that this offering of faith
      is the one unchanging sign
      which links us to ages of Christians,
      past and to come.
      As nations rise and fall,
      as cultures and customs change with the years,
      yet this your sign will ever remain;
      that people will recognize you, the living God,
      in breaking of the bread.
      So we do not approach your table lightly,
      but only in the spirit of faith,
      because you bid us draw near.

17   Since we in the Christian community, O Lord,
     are those who have not seen,
     and yet are called upon to believe this mystery of
     faith,
     send over us, we pray, your Holy Spirit,
     the Spirit who brings us life,
     the Spirit who makes all that we do not easy
     but full of meaning.

18   Only with this help
       can we truly be the Church of Jesus Christ.
       His presence in our community
       gives more than human meaning
       to the support and love we show to one another.
       It is through the Spirit
       that we are united with all people,
       everywhere on this earth.

ALL   **As we believe, so let us live.**
       We pray that all people, looking upon us,
       your Christian community,
       will say in all sincerity,
       'See how they love one another';
       and wherever we have walked,
       the report will go around
       that the poor are clothed,
       the hungry fed,
       the sorrowful comforted,
       and all creation proclaims the wondrous deeds of
       God.
       All these things are possible, Lord God,
       only in Christ,
       and with him and through him. Amen.

*Canon of the Spirit of Justice 47

A eucharistic prayer recalling the presence of Jesus in the marginalized of society.

1   Creator of the world,
     giver of life, spirit of justice,
     thank you for another day of life.
     Thank you for beautiful earth, our home.
     And thank you for giving us the urge to gather
     to recall and celebrate
     and live out your words, your deeds,
     your life among us.
     We acknowledge that not all of life these days
     is going the way that reflects your love.
     Many of your people are homeless,
     hungry, uneducated, unsafe.

2   You call to us again and again,
     from shelters for people who are homeless,
     from hospitals and nursing homes,
     from crack houses,
     from schools and prisons
     and soup kitchens and welfare centres.
     You call to us when you are persecuted
     for being a woman, or a person of colour,
     or poor, or gay or lesbian,
     or mentally handicapped,
     or of an unpopular religion.

ALL   **I was a stranger, and you welcomed me.**

3   We acknowledge
     that much of your suffering in our time
     is caused by systematic neglect
     and the exclusion of many people.
     The institutions of our time,
     government, religion, education,
     insurance and health care,
     often repeat the conspiracy
     that attempted to drive God-with-us
     out of our midst
     two thousand years ago.

ALL   **I was in prison, and you visited me.**

4   But bigotry, cynicism, greed and murder
     did not remove you from your people.
     You promised to stay with us
     even after your execution,
     and you gave us this communal meal
     to refresh and strengthen us.
     You took bread, gave thanks to God,
     blessed it and gave it to us, saying,

ALL   **'Take this, all of you, and eat
     for this is my body.'**

5   Then you took a cup,
     gave thanks, blessed it and gave it to us, saying,

ALL   **'Take this all of you
     and drink from it.
     This is the cup of the new and everlasting covenant.
     It is given for you and for all.
     Do this in memory of me.'**

6   This is the mystery of faith:

**ALL   God with us in this meal.
         God with us in our lives.**

7   Spirit of justice,
     as we eat this bread and drink this cup,
     we will taste the bitterness of injustice
     which crucified Jesus
     and which continues to crucify our sisters and
     brothers.

8   Today we renew our promise to visit you,
     to clothe and to feed you,
     to make sure you are safe for tonight.
     And we renew our promise to help transform our
     society
     into one of liberty
     and of justice for all.

9   As we eat this bread and drink this cup,
     we will taste the sweetness of your life through us,
     with us, in us,
     and we will embody you in our world,
     standing, speaking and acting for justice.

ALL   I was uneducated, and you taught me.

10   Thank you, Creator, Redeemer, Sanctifier of all,
     for the many opportunities we will have today
     and this week
     to be you in our lives.
     We will stretch to fulfil ourselves as your people,
     in solidarity with all of creation,

strong and joyous,
demanders and causers of justice
in the name of Jesus Christ.

ALL   **And it is through Christ,
with Christ, in Christ,
in the unity of the Holy Spirit,
that all honour and glory is yours, almighty Father,
for ever and ever. Amen.**

A modern eucharistic prayer celebrating God's all-embracing love, designed to follow readings and discussion.

1   May God be with you.

℟   **And also with you.**

2   Open your hearts.

℟   **We open them to God and one another.**

3   Let us give thanks to God.

℟   **It is right to give God thanks and praise.**

4   It is right, a good and joyful thing,
        to stand open in the presence of God and one
        another
        as thankful people, lifting our voices in chorus
        with those who have gone before us
        and with men and women throughout the world
        today, saying:

ALL   **Holy, holy, holy God,**
        God of power and might.
        Heaven and earth are full of your glory.
        Hosanna in the highest!
        Blessed is the one who comes in the name of the
        Lord.
        Hosanna in the highest!

5   Wise and gracious God,
Creator of all good things,
Redeemer of this broken world,
you bless your people and the earth itself.

℞   **Holy is your name.**

6   You are the source of love in the world,
the well-spring of justice in history,
the resource of peace on earth.

℞   **Holy is your name.**

7   We pray to you, God of our fathers and mothers,
God of the judges, prophets and priests of Israel,
God of the old covenant and of the new covenant,
God of Mary and Jesus,
God of the Church.

℞   **Holy is your name.**

8   Elohim, you are God.
You lead your people out of bondage into freedom.

℞   **Holy is your name.**

9   Following Jesus, we call you 'Abba', for you love us.
Guiding us, you are insistent,
patient, protective, encouraging, comforting.

℞   **Holy is your name.**

10   God our Father,
your will be done on earth as in heaven.
We thank you for giving us the bread we need.

℞   **Holy is your name.**

11   You hold us in your strong arms like a mother
with her new-born infant.
You have raised your children from generation to
generation,
planting seeds, harvesting grain,
baking fresh bread, preparing meals,
feeding your people,
holding us up when we are too weak to stand on our
own,
teaching us how to walk,
and empowering us to go forth in the world
as your daughters and sons.

℞   **Holy is your name.**

12   God our Mother,
you are the matrix of our power,
our tenderness and our courage.
We forget too often that you are God.

℞   **Holy is your name.**

13   We know that your names are as numerous and
varied as your people,
to whom you reveal yourself in different ways,
so that we may be your co-creative, imaginative
lovers
in a world abundant with redemptive images.

14   We see you in the sun and the moon,
the rain and the wind, coming with power.

15   We see you in the liberation of humanity from injustice and oppression.
We see you coming with power.

16   We see you in our friends and lovers,
      our spouses and children.
      We know your passion, your intensity,
      your commitment to right relationships.
      We experience you coming with power.

17   We see you in the bodies of hungry people, broken
      people, tortured people and a tortured earth.
      We tremble and we believe that you are coming with
      power.

18   We believe in you; we love you;
      we expect you to be with us,
      because we remember the power you revealed to us
      in the life of Jesus, our brother and Christ.

ALL   We remember
      that on the night before he was betrayed
      by those who feared both him and you,
      he ate a Passover meal with his friends,
      in celebration of your liberation of people from
      bondage.

      Remembering your power,
      he took bread, and blessed it,
      and broke it,
      and gave it to his friends, saying,
      'This is my body, which will be broken for you.
      Whenever you eat it, remember me!'

      After supper he took the wine, blessed it,
      and gave it to them, and said,
      'Drink this. This is my blood
      which will be shed for you and for others
      for the forgiveness of sins,
      to heal and empower you.
      Whenever you drink it, remember me.'

Remembering Jesus and the power of your love
revealed through him,
we ask you,
Father and Mother and Friend of all,
to bless this bread and wine,
making it for us the body and blood of Jesus the
Christ.

Bless us also,
that we may be for you
living members of Christ's presence in the world,
people who are in love with you and your creation.

All this we ask in your holy name,
that with Christ and in Christ
and by the power of your Holy Spirit,
we may live for ever as your people,
O gentle God of power and grace. Amen.

49

*Accidents of Birth

A eucharistic liturgy which considers discrimination in our society.

Readings:

1   **Judges 11:30–40**

2   **The Fifth Sense** – a poem by Patricia Beer

> *A 65-year-old Cypriot Greek shepherd, Nicolis Loizou, was wounded by security forces early today. He was challenged twice; when he failed to answer, troops opened fire. A subsequent hospital examination showed that the man was deaf.*
>
> *News item, 30 December 1957.*

Lamps burn all night
Here, where people must be watched and seen,
And I, a shepherd, Nicolis Loizou,
Wish for the dark, for I have been
Sure-footed in the dark, but now my sight
Stumbles among these beds, scattered white boulders,
As I lean towards my far slumbering house
With the night lying upon my shoulders.

My sight was always good,
Better than others. I could taste wine and bread
And name the field they spattered when the harvest
Broke. I could coil in the red
Scent of the fox out of a maze of wood

And grass. I could touch mist, I could touch
breath.
But of my sharp senses I had only four.
The fifth one pinned me to death.

The soldiers must have called
The word they needed: Halt. Not hearing it,
I was their failure, relaxed against the winter
Sky, the flag of their defeat.
With their five senses they could not have told
That I lacked one, and so they had to shoot.
They would fire at a rainbow if it had
A colour less than they were taught.

Christ said that when one sheep
Was lost, the rest meant nothing any more.
Here in this hospital, where others' breathing
Swings like a lantern in the polished floor
And squeezes those who cannot sleep,
I see how precious each thing is, how dear
For I may never touch, smell, taste or see
Again, because I could not hear.

3 **Telephone Conversation** – a poem by Wole Soyinka

The price seemed reasonable, location
Indifferent. The landlady swore she lived
Off premises. Nothing remained
But self-confession. 'Madam,' I warned,
'I hate a wasted journey – I am African.'
Silence. Silenced transmission of
Pressurized good-breeding. Voice, when it came,
Lipstick coated, long gold-rolled
Cigarette-holder pipped. Caught I was, foully.
'HOW DARK?' ... I had not misheard ... 'ARE YOU
LIGHT

OR VERY DARK?' Button B. Button A. Stench
Of rancid breath of public hide-and-speak.
Red booth. Red pillar-box. Red double-tiered
Omnibus squelching tar. It *was* real! Shamed
By ill-mannered silence, surrender
Pushed dumbfoundment to beg simplification.
Considerate she was, varying the emphasis –
'ARE YOU DARK? OR VERY LIGHT?' Revelation
came.
'You mean – like plain or milk chocolate?'

Her assent was clinical, crushing in its light
Impersonality. Rapidly, wave-length adjusted,
I chose. 'West Africa sepia' – and as afterthought,
'Down in my passport.' Silence for spectroscopic
Flight of fancy, till truthfulness changed her accent
Hard on the mouthpiece. 'WHAT'S THAT?'
conceding
'DON'T KNOW WHAT THAT IS.' 'Like brunette.'
'THAT'S DARK, ISN'T IT?' 'Not altogether.
Facially, I am brunette, but, madam, you should see
The rest of me. Palm of my hand, soles of my feet
Are a peroxide blond. Friction, caused –
Foolishly, madam – by sitting down, has turned
My bottom raven black – One moment, madam!' –
sensing
Her receiver rearing on the thunderclap
About my ears – 'Madam,' I pleaded, 'wouldn't you
rather
See for yourself?'

Discussion and prayers

Table blessing:

4   Father of our Lord Jesus Christ,
     in gratitude for the ties that hold us together
     we gather round this table
     mindful of other like-minded groups.

5   Like your people of old
     we are established as many groups
     in a common movement:
     a movement alert to the many ways
     in which your Spirit is ever newly inspiring your
     creation.

6   We wish to remain open to your Spirit's promptings
     from whatever direction they come:
     be they from formal religions and faiths;
     be they from informal groupings that emphasize a
     truth
     that has become stultified in institutionalization;
     or be it from the voice of the secular world.

7   Like your people of old,
     like Moses, like Jesus,
     we walk in the deserts and oases of life.
     Lead us through both!

8   Lead us in the spirit of Jesus,
     who lived to the full each present moment:
     moments of glory; moments of sadness;
     moments of conviction; moments of doubt.

9   Lead us in the spirit of Jesus
who committed himself to you
through his people's and parents' religion
and in his very commitment
went beyond the boundaries of law
to the essence of life-making – that is: love!

ALL   We are here this evening
to celebrate that love,
by doing what Jesus on the eve of his passion
called us to do.

He took bread,
broke it
and gave it to those who were round him saying,
'Take this and eat.
This is my body given for you.'

The bread is passed round.

ALL   Then he took the cup.
Again he thanked and praised you as he said,
'Take this.
Drink from it.
This is my blood, poured out for you.'

The wine is passed round.

10   We ask you to fill our longing
to radiate your love
personified in Jesus.

ALL   In that longing
       we unite ourselves with all Christians
       past present and to come
       as we say
       Our Father,
       who art in heaven ...

11   We hold before you these prayers of ours ...

A time follows for intentions, intercessions, biddings, etc.

12   We commend all these to you as we say:

ALL   The grace of our Lord, Jesus Christ,
       the love of God
       and the fellowship of the Holy Spirit
       be with us all
       now and for ever, Amen.

Other Liturgies

*An Easter Vigil

50

An alternative way of celebrating the night before Easter, at home, with friends.

Introduction and lighting of the candle

After a suitable introduction:

1   And so they left and made the tomb secure
by putting a seal on the stone
and leaving the guard on watch. (Matt. 27:66)

An opportunity for sharing tomb experience follows. As we share, we place dormant 'dead' twigs on the table. Suitable readings follow.

After a time of silence, the fire and Easter candle are lit. We place flowering branches on the table with Easter eggs, as a sign of our hope for a personal experience of resurrection.

Readings

2   Mark 16:1–8

Other suitable readings may follow, and then bidding prayers.

Exsultet and eucharistic prayer

3   Rejoice, heavenly powers!
    Sing, choirs of angels!
    Exult, all creation around God's throne!
    Jesus Christ, our king, is risen!
    Sound the trumpet of salvation!

4   Rejoice, O earth, in shining splendour,
    radiant in the brightness of your king!
    Christ has conquered! Glory fills you!
    Darkness vanishes for ever.

5   Rejoice, community of Christ!
    Exult in glory! The risen Saviour shines upon you!
    Let this place resound with joy
    echoing the mighty song of all God's people.

ALL **This is our Passover feast,
    when Christ, the true lamb, is slain.**

6   This is the night you freed the people of Israel
    from their slavery
    and led them dry-shod through the sea.

ALL **This is the night when we are freed
    and restored to grace.**

7   This is the night when Jesus Christ broke the chains
    of death
    and rose triumphant from the grave.

8   Most blessed of all nights,
    chosen by God to see Christ rising from the dead!

9   The power of this holy night
dispels all evil, takes our guilt away,
restores lost innocence,
brings mourners joy.
It casts out hatred,
brings us peace
and humbles earthly pride.

ALL   May Christ who came back from the dead
shed his light on all humankind.

10   Always, wherever we may be,
we carry with us in our body the death of Christ,
so that the life of Jesus too
may always be seen in our body.

ALL   The night before he died,
Jesus showed how much he loved us.
When he was at supper with his disciples,
he took bread, and gave thanks and praise.
Then he broke the bread,
gave it to his friends and said,
'Take this all of you and eat it.
This is my body which will be given up for you.'

When supper was ended,
Jesus took the cup that was filled with wine.
He thanked you, gave it to his friends, and said,
'Take this, all of you, and drink from it.
This is the cup of my blood,
the blood of the new and everlasting covenant.
It will be shed for you and for all
so that sins may be forgiven.
Do this in memory of me.'

May the light of the risen Christ
dispel the darkness of our hearts and minds.

51

Ecumenical Credo

Written by Dietrich Bonhoeffer, a victim of Nazi persecution, this is his statement of belief, designed to be acceptable to all Christians.

We believe in God, the Father,
Creator of the world,
who made us men and women,
who gave us freedom,
to maintain life,
to promote peace,
to care for our planet
so that all humankind can belong together
in equality and justice.

We believe in Jesus Christ our Lord,
born of Mary as a human being in Israel,
chosen, to bear witness in his life,
to the nearness of God.

He proclaimed the solidarity of God with the poor;
he proclaimed freedom to the imprisoned,
sight to the blind,
amnesty to the oppressed:
he suffered, was tortured
and was executed on the cross under Pontius Pilate,
by those in power,
raised to life and hope for all.
He frees and unites us all throughout the world
without preference,
harmonizing our cultural and political diversities

against all division,
to live with and for one another;
and calls us to a witness of service.

We believe in the Holy Spirit,
the strength of new life in Christ,
who dares us to change – and all circumstances,
who makes us rich with diversity in unity,
who charges us with the task
of bringing all human beings together
in a new community through himself in diversity,
one God, Father, Son and Holy Spirit.

Prayer for Inter-Faith Fellowship 52

Rabbi Simeon Singer's prayer for tolerance of differences in belief and unity in the pursuit of God's will.

God,
your infinite power and wisdom are reflected
in the infinite variety of creation.

We see your work also
in all the differences that are found
in the minds of all the people around us.

We pray to you
for all our brothers and sisters.

Take them all
under the sheltering wing of your love.

Let us see, we pray,
that our many differences of thought and belief
are implanted by you;

and let us strive more zealously
to be one in love and tolerance,
one in the desire
to know and do your will.

53 Prayer for Reconciliation and Unity

A prayer rejoicing in the differences of a common humanity under one God.

1   Let us pray for our reconciliation and unity.

ALL   Lord of all creation,
we stand in awe before you,
impelled by the vision
of the harmony of all people.

We are children of many traditions,
inheritors of shared wisdom
and tragic misunderstandings,
of proud hopes and humble successes.

Now it is time for us to meet,
in memory and truth,
in courage and trust,
in love and promise.

In that which we share,
let us see the common prayer of humanity.

In that in which we differ,
let us wonder at the freedom of humanity.

In our unity and differences,
let us know the uniqueness that is God.

May our courage match our convictions,
and our integrity match our hope.

May our faith in you
bring us closer to each other.

May our meeting with past and present
bring blessing for the future. Amen.

54   A Blessing

A concluding blessing from the Roman Missal.

1   May almighty God bless us in his mercy,
     and make us always aware of his saving wisdom.

℟   **Amen.**

2   May he strengthen our faith with proofs of his love,
     so that we persevere in good works.

℟   **Amen.**

3   May he direct our steps to himself,
     and show us how to walk in charity and peace.

℟   **Amen,**
     and may almighty God bless us,
     the Father, the Son and the Holy Spirit.
     Amen.

Closing Prayer and Blessing 55

A modern closing blessing.

1   Let us pray in thanksgiving.

℞   Lord God, we thank you for calling us
into the company
of those who trust in Christ
and seek to obey his will.

May your Spirit guide and strengthen us
in mission and service to your world;
may we be strangers no longer
but pilgrims on the way to your kingdom.

May the blessing of the Holy Trinity rest upon us
and all our work and worship done in God's name.

And may the grace of our Lord Jesus Christ,
the love of God
and the fellowship of the Holy Spirit
be with us all evermore. Amen.

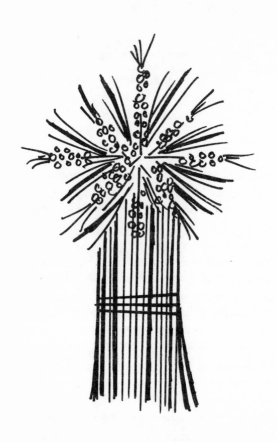

Glossary of Technical Terms

Agape

> The common meal, with at least some liturgical features, of the apostolic Christian community referred to in Acts and 1 Corinthians. Later, as the Love Feast, it was distinguished from the Eucharist.

Anamnesis

> A Greek word expressing the Hebrew concept of memorial, commemoration, remembrance and recalling, but suggesting too that the event commemorated is being made present now.

Anaphora

> A Greek word meaning 'offering', used from a very early date for the eucharistic prayer, the canon or prayer of consecration.

Ashkenazi

> The Jewish tradition of Palestine.

Berakah (plural: Berakoth)

> A Hebrew word meaning a prayer of blessing, giving thanks to God, such as grace before meals. The source of the Christian eucharistic prayer.

Birkat-ha-Mazon

> The Jewish blessing said at the end of the meal over the Cup of Blessing (1 Cor. 10:16), as a thanksgiving for food and for the promised land and a prayer for Jerusalem. (See nos 10, 12, 24 and 28 in this collection.)

Chaburah

> Hebrew 'friend'; a group of friends formed for religious

purposes such as improving observance. Jesus and his disciples constituted such a fellowship and their communal meals were the inspiration for the Eucharist.

Didache

Greek 'teaching'. A short early Christian manual on Church practice, perhaps as early as AD 60 and from an isolated Syrian community. It contains two early accounts of Christian table fellowship or Eucharists. (See nos 15 and 16 in this collection.)

Epiclesis

Greek 'invocation'. Used for the prayer asking the Father to send the Spirit to change the bread and wine into the body and blood of Jesus Christ.

Eucharist

The Greek term for the Hebrew 'Berakah', thus 'thanks-giving'.

Eulogion

Greek 'blessing', used also for the blessed bread distrib-uted after the Eucharist in the Eastern churches.

Haggadah

Hebrew 'narrative', used for parables, legend, folklore and applied particularly to the account of God's saving acts given at the Passover celebration.

Kenosis

Greek 'emptying', referring to God's self-emptying in his acceptance of humanity at the incarnation.

Kiddush

A Hebrew word meaning sanctification, used for the special meal in Jewish homes every Sabbath eve (i.e. Friday evening). At its centre is the Jewish table prayer. (See no. 42 in this collection.)

Moravians

Founded in Bohemia (now in the Czech Republic) in 1457, the Moravians formed their own ministry and left communion with Rome in 1467. Later suppressed, they were revived and flourish still today.

Qedusha

The ancient Hebrew prayer: 'Holy, Holy, Holy is Yahweh of Hosts. The whole earth is full of his glory.'

Qumran

A site some 8 miles south of Jericho at the north-west end of the Dead Sea, occupied at the time of our Lord by an ascetic Jewish community. The Dead Sea scrolls were first discovered there in 1947 and continue to shed light on Jewish belief and practice at the time of the genesis of the Christian Church.

Sanctus

The words 'Holy, Holy, Holy Lord' are taken from the Jewish prayer Qedusha, and frequently open the eucharistic prayer.

Seder

An Ashkenazic term for the ritual of the first night of the Passover. (See no. 43 in this collection.)

Sephardi

The Babylonian Jewish tradition.

Sources and Acknowledgements

It has proved impossible to discover the origins of many of the liturgies in this book. Often they have been through several revisions over the years and those responsible have not been concerned to record their involvement. Apologies are offered where copyright holders detect that we are unaware that their texts have been used. We shall be happy to make full acknowledgement in any future edition.

1   **Prophecies**
    A collection of Jewish prophecies, which Christians believe have been fulfilled by the coming of our Lord and the outpouring of the Spirit on the nations, and which await their consummation at the end of time. These can serve as readings before a Table Liturgy, or as a basis for discussion and Bible study. See also no. 14, A New Covenant Liturgy.

2   **A Preparation**
    From the archives of Catholics for a Changing Church. This originally formed an introduction to no. 36.

3   **Two Acts of Penance**
    From the archives of Catholics for a Changing Church.

4   **Preparation and Kyrie**
    From the archives of Catholics for a Changing Church.

5   **Liturgy of Penance for Sins of Divisiveness**
    From the archives of Catholics for a Changing Church.

6   **Short Liturgy of Reconciliation**
    From the archives of Catholics for a Changing Church.

7 **Liturgy of Hope**
From the archives of Catholics for a Changing Church
and used at a liturgy in October 1993.

8 **Liturgy of Good News**
From the archives of Catholics for a Changing Church.

9 **From the Psalter**
From Psalm 104 (vv. 28–9) but see also Psalm 145 (vv.
16–17), used by many Benedictine communities as a
grace at their meals in common.

10 **The Jewish Blessings**
The first part of the basic table blessing which must have
been part of the prayer of Jesus and his family. A fuller
(and adapted) version is found below as **12 A Table
Blessing** (Berakoth). Compare also nos **24** and **43**. (See
R. C. D. Jasper and G . J. Cuming, *Prayers of the
Eucharist: Early and Reformed* (Pueblo Publishing,
New York, 1987, 3rd rev. edn), p. 10 and Lucien
Deiss, *Springtime of the Liturgy: Liturgical Texts of the
First Four Centuries* (Liturgical Press, Collegeville, MN,
1979), p. 5. Also Louis Bouyer, *Eucharist* (London,
1968), pp. 102–3).

11 **A Community Grace**
Before the Anglican Benedictine community at
Nashdom moved to Elmore in Newbury, this was used as
a blessing before and after meals on some of my visits to
the Abbey in the 1970s and owes much to the Jewish
table blessings. For Christians, all meals are sacra-
mental.

12 **A Table Blessing**
Based on the Jewish table blessing (Berakoth, see no. 10),
this is designed to be as close as possible to what our
Lord may have used, yet harmonized with familiar
modern liturgical texts of the Roman Missal as used in
the UK.

13 **At Table**
This is an interesting example of a table liturgy published by Roman Catholic bishops since the Second Vatican Council (1962–5). From *Catholic Household Blessings and Prayers*, copyright 1988 United States Catholic Conference, Washington DC. Used with permission. Excerpts from the English translation of *Book of Blessings*, 1988, International Committee on English in the Liturgy, Inc. All rights reserved.

14 **A New Covenant Liturgy**
A celebration of the priesthood of all the baptized as fulfilment of Jewish prophecy, combined with the previous liturgy no. 13.

15 **An Early Table Thanksgiving from the *Didache***
This ancient liturgy, discovered in 1875 in a monastery in Constantinople, is here reconstructed (see note on 16 following) and presented in modern English and slightly adapted to conform to familiar liturgical texts. The *Didache* seems to be our earliest Christian liturgical text, perhaps originating in Antioch in Syria in the late first century. It is unclear whether this celebration was intended as a Eucharist or an agape (given a distinction) and even whether one person in fact presided or it was said in common. (Jasper and Cuming, op. cit., p. 23, and Deiss, op. cit., p. 74.)

16 **A Later Table Thanksgiving from the *Didache***
See the note on the previous liturgy. These two forms have been drawn up following the analysis of John Dominic Crossan in *The Historical Jesus, The Life of a Mediterranean Jewish Peasant* (T & T Clark, Edinburgh, 1991), pp. 361–3.

17 **Thanksgiving Meal Prayer**
Tom Stehle of Washington DC provided the text of this

– no wine is needed, just bread. It was originally intended for the annual US Thanksgiving celebration in November, when Americans remember their founding communities. Based on the Didache (see nos 15 and 16 and the Jewish table blessings 10 and 12). Source unknown.

18 **An Agape**
By Warren Talbot, from *Prayers and Poems, Songs and Stories* [no further details available].

19 **Christ's Supper at Cana I**
Adapted from 'The Communion at Sychar' from John Henson, *Other Communions of Jesus*, Stantonbury Parish Print, 1994 (2 Sycamore Street, Taffs Well, Cardiff, CF4 7FU), pp. 77–9.

20 **Christ's Supper at Cana II**
A version of no. 19 prepared by Sister Jo Harvey of Beckenham.

21 **The London Agape**
From the London Agape Group, © John J. Vincent, Ashram Community Trust, first published in *Community Worship*, 1990.

22 **The Journey**
From the archives of Catholics for a Changing Church. Contains a table blessing prepared by Ann Peart, Keith Jenkins and the Congregation of Abraxus.

23 **A Congregational Agape**
From Derek Billings' *Alternative Eucharistic Prayers* (Grove Books, Ridley Hall, Cambridge, CB3 9HU, 1973), p. 23.

24 **Symbols of Communion**
By Malcolm Johnson, from Dr Elizabeth Stuart's *Daring to Speak Love's Name* (Hamish Hamilton, 1992). This is a simplified form of the Jewish table blessings familiar to our Lord. See also nos 10 and 12.

25 **Didsbury Rectory Agape**
From Trevor Lloyd's *Agapes and Informal Eucharists* (Grove Books, Ridley Hall, Cambridge, CB3 9HU, 1973). Slightly modified version as used for an end of term celebration at a College of Education in June 1973.

26 **An Agape on Priesthood**
From the archives of Catholics for a Changing Church (Birmingham group early 1970s).

27 **Institution Narrative**
Jerusalem Bible version of Luke 22, verses 14–20 and a familiar eucharistic acclamation (cf. 1 Cor. 11:26). See also no. **32 From Corinthians.**

28 **The Last Supper**
See 27 **Institution Narrative** and 10 **The Jewish Blessings.**

29 **The Little Gidding Rite**
Part of the Communion service devised by this modern ecumenical community based on that founded by Nicholas Ferrar and George Herbert at Little Gidding in the seventeenth century. John Damian Blackman, formerly of St Augustine's Abbey, Ramsgate (Subiaco Congregation), introduced me to this. (Robert van der Weger *The Little Gidding Prayer Book*, SPCK, 1986, p. 14.)

30 **An Advent Table Liturgy**
Based on a liturgy written by A. W. Shobrook (now Dom Anselm of Alton Abbey) and others of the Birmingham Catholic Renewal Group in 1976.

31 **An Easter Table Liturgy**
Based on a liturgy written by A. W. Shobrook (now Dom Anselm of Alton Abbey) and others of the Birmingham Catholic Renewal Group in 1976.

32 **From Corinthians**
St Paul's account of the early Christian Eucharist, which

is considered to have been written down before the Gospel accounts.

33 **Emmaus Liturgy**
Prepared by Lala Winkley of Catholic Women's Ordination and used at a meeting of the ecumenical network YEAST in October 1995.

34 **An Anaphora for Today**
From the archives of Catholics for a Changing Church.

35 **A Johannine Agape**
From the archives of Catholics for a Changing Church. This is a meditation on the feeding of the five thousand and thus on the Eucharist itself. Note that John 6:51 ('The bread that I shall give is my flesh') has been seen by some scholars as a vestige of a Johannine account of the institution of the Eucharist. Otherwise this liturgy has no formal institution narrative.

36 **Celebrating the Kingdom**
From the archives of Catholics for a Changing Church, normally preceded by no 2.

37 **A Eucharistic Prayer**
From the archives of Catholics for a Changing Church.

38 **Praying for the World**
From the archives of Catholics for a Changing Church.

39 **A Thanksgiving Celebration**
From the archives of Catholics for a Changing Church. Used at a celebration in June 1991 but with a long history as the 'CRM Mass'.

40 **A Eucharistic Thanksgiving**
From the archives of Catholics for a Changing Church.

41 **A Short Canon**
Used by the Catholic Renewal Movement at a liturgy in October 1991. From Janet Morley's *All Desires Known* (SPCK, 1992, used with permission) except for the last

prayer, which is from *In Spirit and in Truth*, Canberra WCC Assembly Worship Book.

42 **A Christian Kiddush**

This is a slightly amended version, incorporating some revisions by Eve Baker, of a text from Wilf and Hilary Fenten of the Catholic Renewal Movement (now Catholics for a Changing Church). It is based on a form of the domestic Jewish rite used on Friday evenings to usher in the Sabbath. (Cf. Lucien Deiss, *Springtime of the Liturgy* (Collegeville, MN, 1979), p. 5.)

43 **A Shorter Christian Seder**

Based on a text prepared and used by friends of the editor, including Tom Stehle, Michael Knight, Jeff Neudorfer and Terry Onderick on a memorable occasion in Virginia in 1990. It is intended to be a modern form of the Chaburah, Jewish fellowship meal, with elements from the Passover Seder and the original Last Supper.

44 **A Simple Communion**

From *Christian Community* Summer 1994 (No. 68) published by NACCAN (the National Association of Christian Communities and Networks).

45 **A CRM Liturgy**

From the archives of Catholics for a Changing Church.

46 **A CRM Canon**

From the archives of Catholics for a Changing Church. Prepared by Cathy Scott for a liturgy in October 1990.

47 **Canon of the Spirit of Justice**

Source unknown, but originally USA. From Peter Lumsden of Catholics for a Changing Church.

48 **An Inclusive Eucharist**

From the archives of Catholics for a Changing Church.

49 **Accidents of Birth**

Prepared by Sister Jo Harvey of Beckenham in 1996.

Other Resources

d'Avila-Latourrette, Victor-Antoine, *Table Blessings*, Ave Maria Press, Notre Dame, Indiana, 1994.

Billings, Derek, *Alternative Eucharistic Prayers*, Grove Books, Nottingham, 1973.

Bishops' Committee on the Liturgy, *Catholic Household Blessings and Prayers*, NCCB/USCC, Washington DC, 1988.

Bronstein, Herbert (ed.), *A Passover Haggadah*, Penguin Books, London, 2nd rev. edn, 1982.

Celebrating One World: a Resource Book on Liturgy & Social Justice, CAFOD/St Thomas More Centre, London, 1987.

Celebrating the Lord's Day, Servant Books, Michigan, 1986.

Cotter, Jim, *Prayer at Night*, Cairns Publications, Sheffield, 1983.

Dale, Alan, *New World*, Oxford University Press, Oxford, 1967.

Dale, Alan, *Winding Quest*, Oxford University Press, Oxford, 1972.

Haas, Harry, *Celebrations*, Sheed & Ward, London, 1969.

Henson, John, *Other Communions of Jesus*, Stantonbury Parish Print, 1994. [2 Sycamore Street, Taffs Well, Cardiff, CF4 7FU]

Huck, Gabe, *Table Prayer Book*, LTP, Chicago, 1980.

In Spirit and in Truth: a Worship Book, WCC, Geneva, 1991.

Lloyd, Trevor, *Agapes and Informal Eucharists*, Grove Books, Nottingham, 1973.

Morley, Janet, *All Desires Known*, MOW/WIT, 1988 (2nd edn SPCK, London, 1992).

Pratt, Oliver & Ianthe, *Christmas and Easter Ideas Book*, Sheed & Ward, London, 1977.

Pratt, Oliver & Ianthe, *Let Liturgy Live*, Sheed & Ward, London, 1973.

Prayers, Poems, Songs and Stories, WCC, Geneva, 1988.

Richards, Hubert, *The Passover Meal*, McCrimmon, Essex, 1990.

St Hilda's Community, *Women Included*, SPCK, London, 1991.

Stuart, Elizabeth, *Daring to Speak Love's Name*, Hamish Hamilton, London, 1992.

The Iona Community Worship Book, Wild Goose Publications, Glasgow, 1988.

The Little Gidding Prayer Book, SPCK, London, 1986.

Tillman, June Boyce, *In Praise of All Encircling Love: inclusive language hymns and prayers*, AIL/Hildegard Press, London, 1992.

Vincent, John (ed.), *Community Worship Revised*, Ashram Community Trust, 1987 [ACT, 239 Abbeyfield Road, Sheffield s4 7aw]

Select Bibliography

The following works will be of interest to those readers who wish to learn more about the theory and history of Christian liturgy.

Bouyer, Louis, *Eucharist* Desclée, Paris, 1966, University of Notre Dame and London, 1968.

Davies, J. G., *A New Westminster Dictionary of Liturgy & Worship*, Westminster Press, Philadelphia, 1986.

Deiss, Lucien, *Springtime of the Liturgy*, Liturgical Press, Collegeville, MN, 1979.

Dix, Dom Gregory, *The Shape of the Liturgy*, A & C Black, London, 1945.

Hebblethwaite, Margaret, 'Basically Ordinary', *Christian Community* No. 68 (Summer 1994, National Association of Christian Communities and Networks).

Jasper, R. C. D. and Cuming, G. J., *Prayers of the Eucharist: Early and Reformed*, Pueblo Publishing Co, NY, 1987.

Jeremias J., *The Eucharistic Words of Jesus*, London, 1975.

Van Gelder, Lambert, 'The New Presider', *De Bazuin*, 8 July 1994 (Utrecht) (ET in *RENEW 92*, Catholics for a Changing Church, London, December 1994).